Five Stars

PROJECT SPONSORS

Missouri Center for the Book

Western Historical Manuscript Collection,
University of Missouri–Columbia

MISSOURI HERITAGE READERS
General Editor, Rebecca B. Schroeder

Each Missouri Heritage Reader explores a particular aspect of the state's rich cultural heritage. Focusing on people, places, historical events, and the details of daily life, these books illustrate the ways in which people from all parts of the world contributed to the development of the state and the region. The books incorporate documentary and oral history, folklore, and informal literature in a way that makes these resources accessible to all Missourians.

Intended primarily for adult new readers, these books will also be invaluable to readers of all ages interested in the cultural and social history of Missouri.

OTHER BOOKS IN THE SERIES

Five Stars

MISSOURI'S MOST FAMOUS GENERALS

James F. Muench

University of Missouri Press
Columbia and London

University of Missouri Press, Columbia, Missouri 65201
Printed and bound in the United States of America
5 4 3 2 1   10 09 08 07 06

Library of Congress Cataloging-in-Publication Data

Muench, James F., 1964–
Five stars: Missouri's most famous generals / James F. Muench.
p. cm. — (Missouri heritage readers)
Summary: "Profiles five U. S. military generals from Missouri: Alexander William
Doniphan, who served in the Mexican-American War; Sterling Price, who served in the
Civil War (Confederate); Ulysses S. Grant, who also served in the Civil War (Union); John
Pershing, who served in WWI; and Omar Bradley, who served in WWII"—Provided by
publisher.
Includes bibliographical references and index.
ISBN-13: 978-0-8262-1656-4 (pbk. : alk. paper)
1. Generals—United States—Biography. 2. Generals—Missouri—Biography. 3. United
States. Army—Biography. 4. Missouri—Biography. I. Title. II. Series.
U52.M84 2006
355.0092'2778—dc22
2006002617

♾™ This paper meets the requirements of the
American National Standard for Permanence of Paper
for Printed Library Materials, Z39.48, 1984.

Designer: Stephanie Foley
Typesetter: foleydesign
Printer and binder: Thomson-Shore, Inc.
Typeface: Adobe Garamond

*Publication of this book has been generously assisted
by a contribution from Sprint Foundation*

This book is dedicated to my wife, Fran,
whose encouragement and patience made this book possible.

It is also dedicated to the love of ideas instilled in my family by
my ancestor Friedrich Muench; to my parents, Laurence and
Esther Muench, who taught me to love history; and to my grand-
parents, Roscoe and Esther Moulthrop, and Albert and Virginia
Muench, whose stories helped make history come alive.

Contents

Acknowledgments

I do not consider myself a historian, certainly nothing more than an amateur in the field. I am a writer who enjoys bringing to life vivid stories in Missouri history.

After researching and writing this book, I have grown to appreciate the efforts of the professional historians whose works I have relied on in gaining my own perspective. Without their tireless efforts to make sense of old, handwritten, often unintelligible documents, this book would not have been possible.

I wish to thank those family members and friends who encouraged and supported me in this endeavor, in particular my wife, Fran, who helped by reading and commenting on the early drafts of each chapter. I also want to thank my mother, Esther, and father, Laurence, who helped develop my love for history. And I want to thank my children, Nolan and April, who put up with my constant urge to improve their knowledge of history at every possible opportunity.

Five Stars

★ ★ ★ ★ ★

1

Introduction

Historians tend to become experts on particular eras, people, or events. This book, however, gives the reader a perspective on the lives of five different men of different eras. This approach inevitably leads to comparisons of their achievements and to the discovery of a continuity in their lives and the wars they fought.

The acclaimed generals on whom this book focuses—Alexander William Doniphan, Sterling Price, Ulysses S. Grant, John J. Pershing, and Omar Bradley—are five in a long line of men and women from Missouri who have served in the nation's armed services. There were approximately thirty who had a strong connection to Missouri, about twenty of whom were involved in the Civil War.

Although all five generals stand out in their achievements and captured the public's imagination, four other Missouri generals also deserve recognition but could not be included in this work: Civil War generals John Pope and William Tecumseh Sherman; Enoch Crowder, who drafted the first selective service law during World War I; and General Maxwell Taylor, who served with great distinction in World War II, Korea, and Vietnam.

After his early successes in Missouri in the capture of New Madrid and Island No. 10, and perhaps through his friendship with Abraham Lincoln, John Pope received command of the Army of the Potomac in the Civil War. After losing the Second Battle of Bull Run in August

1862, he was assigned to several posts in the West and became a successful Indian fighter and a strong advocate for changes in U.S. policy toward Native Americans. He returned to St. Louis in 1865 and assumed command of troops from Arkansas to Minnesota. This was the second-largest geographical area commanded by a U.S. general at the time.

During the Civil War, General Grant relied on William T. Sherman as his chief subordinate commander, and afterward Sherman became President Grant's army chief of staff. He was especially well known for his "war of movement" theory, which was later used by Pershing and Bradley on the battlefields of World War I and World War II. Sherman and Pope are buried in St. Louis.

Enoch H. Crowder served as the army's judge advocate general and as ambassador to Cuba. He drafted the selective service law that built the military forces needed to defeat the Central powers in World War I. Throughout the latter half of the twentieth century, this military draft legislation played an important role in providing manpower for the nation's armed forces.

Born within thirty miles of the birthplace of Pershing and Bradley, Maxwell Taylor was General Matthew Ridgway's chief of staff for the Eighty-second Airborne Division. In World War II, Taylor was the first American general to land in France during the D-day invasion, and he commanded the 101st Airborne during the siege of Bastogne at the height of the Battle of the Bulge. He commanded the Eighth Army in the Korean War and served as army chief of staff in the late 1950s and as chairman of the Joint Chiefs of Staff in the 1960s. During the Cold War, Taylor advocated a more "flexible response" to the Soviet threat, advising the deployment of strong conventional forces rather than subscribing to the prevailing doctrine of "massive retaliation," which would have employed nuclear weapons.

Historically, Missouri generals have come from rural backgrounds. Even after Missouri became a state in 1821, it was the frontier, and throughout most of its history the state's economy has relied heavily on agriculture. Doniphan was a country lawyer, Price and Grant were farmers, Pershing was a rural schoolteacher, and Bradley was the son of a rural schoolteacher. The military was a way for rural boys to escape poverty. For families lacking money for higher education, such as the Pershings and Bradleys, the military academy at West Point was seen as an inexpensive avenue to an education.

Before the Civil War, generals tended to be citizen soldiers or, as in the case of William Doniphan and Sterling Price, political leaders volunteering for military service. During the Civil War, and afterward, professional military leadership became more important to success on the battlefield. In the twentieth century, with the growth of a professional military, generals increasingly took on the role of managers: they were no longer merely inspiring figures who led the charge. John Pershing laid the foundation for this change, and Omar Bradley and other Pershing successors refined the role.

Although the state's military leaders exhibit great variety in personality and accomplishment, there is a common thread that binds the best of them together—a can-do attitude derived from Missouri's frontier past that displays itself in the practical idea that results matter most. When Napoleon was asked to name the generals he considered greatest, he said, "The victors." Missouri's generals have understood the basic maxim that a general must, first and foremost, win battles.

The can-do spirit, with its focus on results, was evident during Alexander Doniphan's epic march into Mexico in 1846 and during Pershing's drive to the Marne in World War I. Both of these generals pushed their soldiers to achieve the impossible. Doniphan drove his men to victory against larger enemy forces while enduring extreme hardships: exposure to harsh weather, hazardous terrain, and lack of food, water, and clothing. Pershing pushed his men to advance up San Juan Hill in Cuba during the Spanish-American War under a heavy barrage of enemy bullets, and he pressed men through deadly machine gun and artillery fire to finally break the stalemate on the western front in World War I. Grant pushed his men to keep fighting at Shiloh and in the Wilderness campaign and through sieges at Vicksburg and Petersburg, even when victory seemed extremely uncertain. The can-do spirit also shows when a military situation looks bleak, as it did for Bradley during Hitler's last gasp in the Battle of the Bulge. Although surprised by the enemy, Bradley stood his ground and found a way to win, turning misfortune into victory.

The can-do spirit also comes through when a general chooses to gamble, as Price gambled on a raid into Missouri late in the Civil

War. If it had worked, it might have saved the Confederacy or at least prolonged its survival. Similarly, Bradley and his superiors had to gamble on the D-day invasion of France in World War II. If the invasion had been stymied at the Normandy beaches, as it nearly was at Omaha, the war might have lasted several more years, and Hitler might have won.

The can-do spirit comes through when a commander comes up with a very practical and inventive tactic such as Doniphan's at the battle of El Brazito. The amateur general, knowing the range of the Mexican muskets, lured the enemy into range by ordering his men to fall as if they had been hit, and then to stand and surprise the enemy with a devastating barrage of gunfire to win the battle. This was frontier trickery at its best.

The can-do spirit is rooted in the practical rural culture from which many Missouri generals have sprung. Far from the city, and unable to get help quickly, settlers learned to rely on themselves and make do, finding workable ways to get around problems. In fact, the best Missouri generals were practical men who learned much in practical jobs. Pershing and Grant, for instance, both served as quartermasters early in their careers, gaining valuable experience in the importance of keeping their men fed and supplied.

The can-do spirit goes hand in hand with the volunteer tradition of Missouri generals, good citizens putting aside the plow to carry a rifle in defense of their country. Even as the need for professionalism grew in importance in modern warfare, especially during and after the Civil War, the volunteer spirit still was important in building the armies needed to succeed on the battlefield. Training had always been important, whether, as in Doniphan's case, it was gained by studying military books or learned at West Point. But it became even more necessary with the advent of more powerful and technological weapons. Generals had to learn to operate on the battlefield in ways that would counteract the latest efficient killing machine. In the years following the Civil War, events on the international stage would also point to the need for a professional military. The rapid-fire successes produced by the Prussian war machine against the Austrians in 1866 and the French in 1870 were evidence enough. To compete on the world stage, the United States would need a similar system.

Missourians can take pride in their state's history of producing a host of noteworthy military leaders who gained fame across the nation. Their lives are worthy of study for anyone interested in their achievements and their contributions to history, and for those interested in learning how to be successful leaders. There is no better way to learn lessons in practical leadership than by studying the lives of successful leaders of the past.

2

Alexander W. Doniphan

Alexander William Doniphan came to Missouri in 1830, a young lawyer seeking his fortune on the frontier. He would later become a national hero by leading Missouri volunteer troops to victory in the Mexican War and would leave an enduring legal document in a new law code for the New Mexico Territory.

If the Civil War had not come after the acclaimed feats of his Missouri Volunteers in the earlier war, Doniphan might still be remembered as one of our greatest national military and political heroes. But because he failed to choose sides during Missouri's secession crisis before the Civil War, he was relegated to the political sidelines. If it is true, as Ulysses S. Grant said in his memoirs, that the seeds of the Civil War were planted in the Mexican War, then it might also be said that in some ways the seeds of Doniphan's political decline were sown during his crowning success, his epic march into Mexico.

The life of the man who marched his men thousands of miles, conquered New Mexico without a shot, and then reinvented its government began rather simply. Will Doniphan was born July 9, 1808, in Mason County, Kentucky. His father, Joseph Doniphan, was a Revolutionary War veteran who had followed Daniel Boone through the Cumberland Gap to Boonesboro, Kentucky. After his father died in 1813, his mother sent him to live with his oldest

Alexander Doniphan, *ca.* 1847. This engraving appeared in the 1847 account of Doniphan's expedition by John T. Hughes. (State Historical Society of Missouri, Columbia.)

brother in Augusta, Kentucky, so that he could attend school. At the age of fourteen, he entered Augusta College and graduated four years later, having developed a talent for rhetoric and oratory.

In 1827, after taking several months to study English literature, Doniphan began reading law as an apprentice in the office of Martin Marshall, the brother of Supreme Court justice John Marshall. Two years later, he joined the Kentucky and Ohio bar associations before following the wanderlust path of his father and migrating west to the Missouri frontier.

Doniphan began practicing law in Lexington, in Lafayette County, but he moved farther west in May 1833 to Liberty, in Clay County, where he shared a law office with David Rice Atchison. Atchison had been practicing law in Liberty for a few years and sent some casework Doniphan's way. He would become Doniphan's good friend and chief political opponent as the Civil War approached.

Doniphan enjoyed spending his leisure time with Atchison, hunting and fishing, playing cards, gambling, horse racing, and attending parties and political events. He also joined Atchison's volunteer militia company, the Liberty Blues. The company gathered three times a year to drill, picnic, and drink. He saw his first military action as a private and aide to Colonel Samuel C. Allen when the Blues were called to serve in the Heatherly War, an eighteen-day event in 1836 that was not much of a war. The conflict was sparked by rumors that two white men had been murdered by Indians in a sparsely populated area of northwestern Missouri. Fearing a possible Indian uprising, the governor called up five companies of state militia, about 200 men, to march along Missouri's western border to look for marauding natives. There were none to be found.

Lieutenant Colonel Stephen Watts Kearny, under whom Doniphan would serve in the Mexican War, also investigated the incident, leading a force of U.S. troops from Fort Leavenworth. Kearny discovered that the killings had occurred after a local gang of thieves led by the Heatherly brothers tried to sell whiskey to a Potawatomi hunting party in the Platte country. After the brothers stole the Indians' horses during the night, the Potawatomis tracked the horses into Missouri and battled with the Heatherly gang, killing three of them.

Acting under the direction of "Old Mother" Heatherly, the brains of the outfit, the gang had taken full advantage of the situation by creating false rumors about Indians on the warpath to raise fear across the countryside. During the excitement, the Heatherlys robbed and killed two men and blamed the murders on the Indians. Once their plot was discovered, the Heatherly gang was arrested, tried, and sent to jail.

Perhaps the most important formative events for Doniphan, however, were his dealings with and for the Mormons in western Missouri. Doniphan's law career was forged in his defense of Mormons who began settling in Jackson County in 1831, on land that is now part of the Kansas City metropolitan area. By 1833, there were about 1,200 members of the Church of Jesus Christ of Latter Day Saints who had settled in the area.

As more and more Mormon settlers arrived, their neighbors grew alarmed. Joseph Smith Jr., the Mormon prophet, and other church leaders believed their church was destined to create a religious community in western Missouri from which Christ, in his Second Coming, would rule the world. Smith's neighbors were disturbed by his denunciation of slavery and feared that Mormon beliefs and social practices, including polygamy, would infect the region. Concerned that the sect would gain control of Jackson County, in 1833 a large force of determined Jackson Countians drove them from their homes, engaging in the type of vigilante violence they would later employ in the border war with Kansas. Angry neighbors attacked the Mormons, tearing down their houses, beating their men, and threatening their women and children with death if they did not leave. The Mormons fought back. Two Jackson Countians and one Mormon died in a major skirmish.

After appealing to the governor without success, the Mormons asked Doniphan, Atchison, and two other local lawyers to represent church members in court. Although he did not agree with the Mormons' beliefs, Doniphan decided to represent them because they were a persecuted minority, and because he strongly believed violence could not be tolerated in a republic based on the rule of law. The four lawyers received an extraordinary fee of $1,000 from the Mormons; the attorneys knew they would lose other local business if they took the case.

Governor Daniel Dunklin called out the Missouri militia to disarm the Mormons and force them to leave Jackson County, appointing Judge John F. Ryland of Lexington, Missouri, to conduct an investigation into the incidents. The Mormons headed northward into Clay, Ray, Lafayette, and Van Buren counties, but they refused to give up their property in Jackson County, even though a Jackson County delegation offered to buy it for more than its appraised value. Mormon leaders would not allow Doniphan and his team of attorneys to compromise on this point.

The lawyers on both sides agreed to schedule court hearings in Independence after a three-month cooling-off period. Dunklin called on Atchison's militia unit to provide protection for the Mormons, so Atchison turned the Mormon legal defense over to Doniphan. The militia brought the Mormon witnesses into Independence, but after an angry mob assembled for the hearing, the judge decided to postpone the trial indefinitely.

Doniphan filed a continuance until the fall and then asked for a change of venue for the next spring. The Missouri Supreme Court would eventually decide the legal case against the Mormons in 1839 after the "Mormon War." Blaming church members for the conflict, the state of Missouri forced them to sign over all their lands to pay for the mustering of the state militia and gave them a few months to leave Missouri.

Meanwhile, Doniphan tried mediation. In 1834 Mormon leader Joseph Smith arrived from the East with Zion's Camp, a paramilitary group, to reinstall the Mormons on their Jackson County property by force. At a meeting on June 16, 1834, Judge Ryland attempted to forge a compromise, hoping that Jackson Countians would purchase the Mormon land and pay reparations to the church, but the Mormons refused to sell their property, and all other attempts at compromise failed.

Although his defense of the Mormons was unsuccessful, the church considered Doniphan a friend for life, and his stature in the area rose even though many residents did not support the Mormons. He earned a reputation as a champion of democratic values for protecting the minority group and for trying to reach a compromise to keep the peace.

The Mormon case publicized Doniphan's legal skills and helped build his law business. He tried cases involving all sorts of disputes over debts, land, and property, as well as criminal cases. He usually won, often because of his great skill as an orator. During his law career, he defended 188 people accused of murder, and in his later years, he expressed regret that he may have helped some guilty people escape the noose.

Doniphan was known as a lawyer who was willing to help downtrodden people achieve justice, and some of his cases involved runaway slaves or free blacks. In one case, Doniphan helped a slave who had been freed upon his owner's death. The owner's heirs had wanted to keep him a slave. Like most southerners, he supported slavery as a "necessary" institution. As a child, Doniphan had received a slave in his father's will, and he owned a handful of slaves throughout his life. Having grown up with the institution, it seemed natural to him, but he appears to have been relatively compassionate to enslaved African Americans.

Biographer Roger D. Launius noted that Doniphan was considered

First Discussion of the Platte Purchase, a mural in the Missouri State Capitol, painted by Walter Ufer, shows a speaker at a militia muster in Liberty in 1835. Doniphan was involved in the negotiations in which Indian tribes turned over two million acres of land to the United States. The Platte Purchase became part of Missouri, later forming Platte, Buchanan, Andrew, Holt, Nodaway, and Atchison counties. (Ralph W. Walker, courtesy State Historical Society of Missouri, Columbia.)

to be a great debater but not a great legal scholar. He impressed juries and won clients with his entertaining and energetic speaking style, not with his knowledge of the finer points of the law. His lucrative law practice allowed him to try other business ventures, such as investment in real estate in western Missouri, and he became involved in the effort to annex the Platte country, now Missouri's northwestern triangle. As a member of the Missouri House of Representatives, to which he was elected in 1836, Doniphan served on a committee that steered the annexation through the legislature. President Martin Van Buren gave it final approval in 1837.

Doniphan had joined the Whig Party in 1836. The party, which developed from a coalition of people who did not like the policies of President Andrew Jackson, was led nationally by Kentucky senator Henry Clay, who became Doniphan's idol. Jacksonian Democrats, such as Missouri senator Thomas Hart Benton, stood for the common man's ability to solve his own problems without interference from government. Whigs, on the other hand, believed government should invest in building economic infrastructure. For instance, shortly after President Jackson's battle to shut down the Bank of the United States on the national level, Doniphan supported the opening of a state bank.

Still trying to help the Mormons, one of Doniphan's legislative projects was to create a homeland for them that would allow them to remain separate from other citizens. Many Mormons had settled in Doniphan's Clay County after their removal from Jackson County. As their numbers grew, Clay Countians began to resist their settlement just as the Jackson Countians had a few years earlier.

Doniphan worked to have the Mormons settled in the new county of Caldwell, which had been carved from an unpopulated section of Ray County, establishing a sort of reservation for Mormons where they would have their own jurisdiction. The Mormons set up a new settlement in Caldwell County called Far West.

Thinking that he had settled the Mormon issue, Doniphan did not run for reelection in 1838. He had fallen in love with a young woman from a well-known local family. On December 21, 1837, he married Elizabeth Jane Thornton, the seventeen-year-old daughter of John Thornton, a fellow state legislator from Clay County.

Although his wife had only an elementary education, Doniphan and Elizabeth had common interests and often read books together. He was twelve years older, but he appears to have truly enjoyed his wife's company. He would often sacrifice his political aspirations to be with her. In 1838, he returned to practicing law, and later that year, his wife gave birth to a boy, John Thornton. Two years later, she had a second son, Alexander William Jr.

Little did Doniphan know that his Mormon solution would soon collapse, and that his military career would begin in earnest. Life had been peaceful in the newly created Caldwell County, with its 10,000 citizens and Far West as its county seat. Mormons controlled the county government and operated their own state militia company. But trouble arose as more Mormon immigrants arrived and began to settle in areas outside the borders of Caldwell County, in violation of an unwritten agreement not to do so.

In addition, a new movement within the Mormon church was

FIGHT AT GALLATIN, MISSOURI, BETWEEN MORMONS AND "GENTILES."

Trouble between Missourians and Mormon settlers developed at Gallatin, Missouri, when the Mormons, who had settled primarily in Caldwell County, spread beyond Caldwell and tried to settle and vote in Daviess County. (State Historical Society of Missouri, Columbia.)

violently expelling members who disagreed with the church leadership. When vigilantes, known as Danites, removed several church members from the Far West settlement, those evicted warned the public that the church's new militancy was a threat to other citizens. Violence erupted during an election on August 6, 1838, in the town of Gallatin in Daviess County, the adjoining county to the north of Caldwell. A group of non-Mormons rioted and forcibly prevented a group of Mormons from voting.

Incensed, Mormon leader Joseph Smith led an armed contingent of Mormons to Adam-ondi-Ahman, the chief Mormon settlement in Daviess County. Under an implied threat of violence, a local judge signed a statement supporting the Mormons, but, as soon as they left, he charged Smith with trying to start a war.

A warrant was issued for the arrest of Smith and his chief lieutenant, and Smith asked Doniphan and Atchison to represent them. The lawyers agreed and convinced Smith and his lieutenant to surrender. A hearing was held September 7, after which the defendants were ordered to appear before a grand jury.

Within days, tensions boiled over again when the Mormon militia captured three men running guns to the anti-Mormon faction in Daviess County. A Mormon court held the men for trial while both sides appealed to the governor. A judge ordered the Mormons to free the prisoners and asked Atchison to send a militia force to diffuse the situation. Atchison appointed Doniphan to the rank of brigadier general and put him in charge of 200 state militia soldiers from Clay County.

Five days after the hearing for Smith and his lieutenant, Doniphan marched his troops to the border between Clay and Caldwell counties, where they camped near the Crooked River. He rode to Far West and persuaded the Mormons to turn over the alleged gunrunners and their weapons to him. After delivering the prisoners and guns to his friend Atchison, Doniphan moved north into Daviess County and placed his army between the Mormon settlement and a gathering force of anti-Mormons near Gallatin, where Atchison joined him. Doniphan and Atchison managed to convince the opposing forces to go home.

After representing a group of Mormons accused of rioting at a hearing in Daviess County, Doniphan and Atchison told the governor that the problems in western Missouri could quickly flare again at the slightest provocation. Nevertheless, the governor sent the militia home.

As Doniphan had predicted, within days the Mormons and their enemies were at each other's throats again, and the militia was called up once more. The Mormons fortified Adam-ondi-Ahman, and Joseph Smith sent 400 Mormon soldiers from Far West to the settlement. On October 18, 1838, the Mormon soldiers sacked and burned the Daviess County towns of Gallatin and Millport and burned down some farmhouses.

Doniphan raised a new state militia and headed to Far West to negotiate with the Mormons, who were already sending more men into Daviess County. Meanwhile, another militia unit from Clay County under Captain Samuel Bogart, on patrol at the Caldwell-Ray county line, exceeded orders and forcibly disarmed Mormons in both counties. On October 24, Bogart's men captured two Mormon spies in Ray County and took them to his camp. Mormon troops tried to rescue the prisoners the next day and touched off a skirmish. Three Mormons and one of Bogart's men were killed.

It was the last straw for Governor Lilburn Boggs, who ordered Major General John B. Clark to lead 2,000 militiamen against the Mormons. The governor then issued his infamous "Extermination Order" of October 27, 1838, in which he decreed, "The Mormons must be treated as enemies, and must be exterminated or driven from the State if necessary for the public peace—their outrages are beyond all description."

The governor then placed Doniphan under Clark's command, in effect firing Atchison because of the lawyer's sympathy for the Mormons. When Doniphan learned of Atchison's removal on October 28, he considered resigning, but Atchison suggested he keep his command to protect the Mormons from bloodshed.

The next day Doniphan marched the 2,000 men he and Atchison had assembled to Far West, to which most of the Mormons had retreated after hearing of Governor Boggs's order. Arriving on October 30, Doniphan set up lines of defense and prepared for battle. Mormon leader Joseph Smith sent a message to Doniphan offering to compromise, and Doniphan agreed to meet him the next morning.

In the morning, Colonel George M. Hinkle, commander of the Mormon Caldwell County militia, came forward to negotiate a peace treaty. But the senior state militia general on the scene, Samuel D. Lucas of Jackson County, gave the Mormons an hour to surrender and told them that if they refused to surrender, they would face extermination. Hinkle convinced him to give the Mormons twenty-four hours to surrender by promising that the Mormon leadership would give themselves up as hostages.

When Joseph Smith and his lieutenants surrendered to the state militia, the Missouri troops roughed them up and taunted them, and some even threatened to shoot them. Doniphan and other officers surrounded Smith and his men, protecting them with drawn swords until the swarm of angry militiamen backed off.

The following morning, General Lucas accepted the surrender of 600 Mormon soldiers. As a slight to Lucas, Hinkle handed over his sword and pistols to Doniphan. Lucas then ordered his men to take control of Far West and to search for more weapons. The Mormons later accused the Missourians of spending days plundering and committing acts of violence and rape.

That evening, Lucas presided over a court-martial of the Mormon leaders. Smith and his six lieutenants were convicted of treason and sentenced to death. Doniphan argued vigorously that the men should be turned over to civilian authorities, but he was outvoted by a majority of the other officers. He argued that the court-martial was "illegal as hell" because the defendants were not all members of the militia and therefore not subject to military law. Moreover, the governor had not declared martial law; therefore the accused Mormons should have been tried in a civil court, not in a military court. The court-martial proceeding illegally removed their constitutional right to due process.

When the guilty verdict was announced, Doniphan stood and said that neither he nor his brigade would have anything to do with such cold-blooded murder, and he ordered his men to prepare to march away. But Lucas wouldn't let him go so easily. At midnight, he sent Doniphan an order to shoot Joseph Smith and the other prisoners in the Far West public square at 9 a.m.

Doniphan responded in writing that he would not obey an order to commit cold-blooded murder, swearing before God that if Lucas executed the Mormons, he would hold him responsible in court. According to biographer Roger Launius, Doniphan told Lucas privately, "You hurt one of these men if you dare and I will hold you personally responsible for it, and at some other time you and I will meet again when in mortal combat and we will see who is the better man."

In the morning, Doniphan gathered his troops and ceremoniously marched them past the Mormon prisoners. In full view of Lucas, he reputedly called out to the prisoners, "By God, you have been sentenced by the court-martial to be shot this morning; but I will be damned if I have any of the honor of it, or any of the disgrace of it, therefore I have ordered my brigade to take up the line of march and to leave the camp, for I consider it to be cold-blooded murder, and I bid you farewell."

Doniphan's mutiny, with the clear statement of his motive, caused Lucas to lose his nerve. Instead of executing the prisoners, he sent them to Independence, Missouri, to be tried by civilian authorities. Lucas ordered the rest of the Mormons to leave the state immediately.

Mustering out of the militia on November 5, Doniphan later that month defended the Mormons and got twenty-nine defendants freed for lack of evidence. Five others, including Joseph Smith, were held to await trial for murders committed during the shoot-out at Crooked River. Twenty-four more were bound over for trial on suspicion of criminal activity but were released on bail and fled the state quickly, as had been expected.

Doniphan was unsuccessful in getting the five Mormon leaders released. They were held in jail over the winter, brought before a grand jury on April 6, 1839, and were indicted on April 11 for crimes in Daviess County but granted a change of venue to Boone County. After months of trying, Doniphan had finally arranged for the trial to be moved. On the way to Boone County, the sheriff and deputies guarding the Mormons supposedly got drunk and fell asleep, allowing the Mormons to escape. After another group of Mormons broke out of the Columbia jail, many observers began to suspect that state officials had engineered the escapes as a way to end the episode.

In 1840, Doniphan won reelection to a second term in the state legislature. According to historian Perry McCandless, a Mormon official had deeded "slightly over 1,000 acres" in Jackson County to him in 1838 in payment for his work. The Mormons moved on to Nauvoo, Illinois, and eventually to Utah. Those who remained in Kansas City formed the Reorganized Church of Jesus Christ of Latter Day Saints, recently renamed the Community of Christ.

On June 25, 1976, nearly 140 years later, Missouri governor Christopher S. Bond issued an executive order rescinding Governor Boggs's Extermination Order of October 27, 1838.

★

Doniphan's ability to forge compromise and to form consensus between opposing points of view was an important asset on the frontier, where people needed to rely on each other to survive. Men and women of principle had to find a way to work together even when their principles clashed. Such tactics had helped mediate the conflict with the Mormons in northwest Missouri, and Doniphan's talents in the diplomatic arena would be useful during the coming conflict with Mexico and the integration of the former Mexican territories in the Southwest into the United States.

But first, Doniphan would lead his Mexican War regiment on an amazing 5,500 mile march from Missouri through the Southwest and into Mexico. His exploits during this trek made him a legend, and his march into Mexico evoked comparisons by newspapers to Xenophon's march across Asia Minor, Alexander the Great's march from Macedonia to India, and Hannibal's march over the Alps.

The conflict with Mexico began in 1835, when Texas declared its independence from Mexico. Doniphan was a member of the Whig Party, but, like most Missourians, he supported the annexation of Texas, although most Whigs and their champion, Senator Henry Clay, and even the Democratic senator from Missouri, Thomas Hart Benton, did not. When Democrat James K. Polk was elected president in 1844, Texas annexation gained support. Just before Polk took office in 1845, Congress passed a resolution for the annexation, but Mexico still had not recognized the independence of Texas. Its annexation by the United States meant war.

In the middle of May 1846, Missouri governor John C. Edwards asked Doniphan to put together a cavalry unit to meet the presidential call for volunteers to fight in Mexico. Doniphan recruited 120 men, mostly from Clay County. In June 1846, he marched his men to Fort Leavenworth to join Colonel Stephen Watts Kearny's Army of the West. The Missouri regiment grew to 856 men within a couple of weeks.

Kearny, a regular army officer who would soon be promoted to brigadier general, and his West Point officers whipped Doniphan's regiment into shape. The regulars looked down on the volunteers because they were often unkempt and tended not to take to military discipline. At that time, volunteer companies selected their own officers. Doniphan had enlisted as a private, but the regiment elected him colonel partly because of the overall contempt for military discipline he had stressed in his campaign to garner votes. Colonel would be his official rank in the U.S. Army, even though he was a brigadier general in the Missouri state militia.

Kearny explained the mission to Doniphan and gave him books

on tactics, which Doniphan studied at the fort and during the march into Mexican territory. Along with Kearny's regular forces, units of the First Missouri Volunteers began leaving Fort Leavenworth on June 22, 1846, heading west on the Santa Fe Trail toward a rendezvous 565 miles away at Bent's Fort. They marched twenty to twenty-five miles a day. The trek across the plains was difficult with hot sun that delivered sunburns and chapped lips, and the farther they walked, the more ragged their clothes became. Worst of all, supply problems dogged them, and they found themselves on the brink of starvation several times. Luckily, when they reached the Arkansas River on July 12, they found plenty of buffalo and abundant, although muddy, water.

By July 20, they had crossed the Arkansas River, and Doniphan, at Kearny's direction, was pushing his men to march twenty-five to twenty-eight miles a day in 100-degree heat. Some of the men almost mutinied. Kearny urged Doniphan to enforce stricter military discipline, but Doniphan refused, saying he didn't want to break the men. Kearny warned Doniphan that he would be held responsible for the conduct of his soldiers, but he would later admit that Doniphan had been right. According to Roger Launius, Kearny commended Doniphan's judgment and "measured all the other non-regular army units he dealt with during the Mexican War by the Missourians' example."

The main body of Doniphan's troops reached Bent's Fort, near what is now Pueblo, Colorado, on July 28. Built by the commercial firm of Bent and St. Vrain, it was a trading post, an oasis of civilization, and a crossroads for trappers, traders, and Indians, and now it would become a launching pad for the invasion into Mexican territory.

On August 2, Kearny sent ahead to Santa Fe a detachment of dragoons—mounted soldiers—to inform Mexican governor Don Manuel Armijo that the United States had annexed the province of New Mexico and that the governor would be held responsible if he opposed the annexation. It appears they may have bribed Armijo with property and money in return for his compliance in the annexation.

Kearny then ordered Doniphan to push on to Santa Fe. Doniphan's soldiers had thought the trip to Bent's Fort was tough, but this march was more difficult, over the forbidding hot, dry terrain known as the Great American Desert. The Missourians were happy to reach the Purgatoire River, where they received a day off to recuperate before taking on the Raton Pass, one of the steepest and most rugged mountain crossings in North America.

As they struggled up to a height of 7,754 feet above sea level, Doniphan cut the men's rations to half, and then to a third. By the time they reached the first Mexican settlements in New Mexico, a week after leaving Bent's Fort, their horses were dying of exhaustion and many of the men were on foot.

The night before they entered Las Vegas, New Mexico, the first village of any particular size, Kearny asked Doniphan for legal advice about how best to interpret his orders to take possession of the territories of New Mexico and California and to naturalize the residents as U.S. citizens. Doniphan recommended that Kearny make the Mexicans take an oath of loyalty to the United States, a policy Kearny followed throughout their tour of the newly annexed towns of New Mexico. The next day, August 14, they occupied Las Vegas without opposition.

Advancing southward toward Santa Fe, the men expected the Mexican army to attack at any minute. An ambush at Apache Canyon seemed likely, but none came. They found some Mexican cannons in the canyon, but the soldiers who had manned the guns had retreated.

Fortunately, Kearny's advance negotiators had done their job well. Kearny and Doniphan's army was small and tired, and they were in hostile territory, thousands of miles from home. Their regiments were running low on supplies and were relatively unprepared for a fight. A Mexican battalion could have easily defeated the U.S. forces if it had caught them in the right place at the right time or if a small force had engaged the Americans in a long, drawn out fight until more Mexican troops arrived. Thankfully, though, the Americans were able to bribe the Mexican governor and to deal with the local Mexican business leaders, and Santa Fe was captured without a shot. Governor Armijo abdicated and retreated to the Mexican province of Chihuahua.

For the next two months, while in Santa Fe, Doniphan dealt with squabbles between regulars and volunteers and built Fort Marcy, overlooking Santa Fe. Most important, at Kearny's order, he began to establish a new government and law code for the conquered province. Using a handful of law books, Doniphan led a small committee that melded Spanish colonial, Mexican, and English common law systems into what would become known as the Kearny Code. Doniphan presented it to General Kearny for approval on September 21, 1846.

Translating laws from Spanish and adapting them to conform to the U.S. Constitution and the Northwest Ordinance for territorial governments was difficult. The code established an executive branch with a governor and a secretary, an elected legislative branch, and a supreme court with three justices. Congress would later criticize Kearny for overstepping his authority by creating a civil government and appointing its officials. The code, however, quickly brought a democratic government to the New Mexico Territory.

With a new government in place, Kearny and his army regulars left on September 25 for California, leaving Doniphan in charge. He was to serve as the territorial military commander until Sterling Price and his reinforcements arrived from Fort Leavenworth. Price's forces straggled into Santa Fe during the next few weeks, and, as soon as he was relieved by Price, Doniphan was ready to head south into Mexico. But first he would have to calm Navajo unrest.

Native American raids, in this case by Utes, Apaches, and Navajos, had been a constant problem for Mexican and American settlers. While Kearny's army was invading New Mexico, the Navajos had mounted a raid and carried off twenty Mexican families. While in Santa Fe, Kearny, and then Doniphan, negotiated with all three tribes, but it became clear that trouble was brewing.

The arrival of Price, whose troops could now garrison Santa Fe and other settlements, allowed Doniphan to be more active with his men. On October 2, Kearny sent an order to Doniphan to attack the Navajos in retaliation for killing several New Mexican shepherds. Navajo warriors appeared to be testing the new American defenses, and Kearny thought their actions required a strong response.

After signing a peace treaty with the Utes, Doniphan headed out with three companies of men into Navajo territory, looking for trouble but finding mainly abandoned hogans. Eventually, however, an aging Navajo emissary told Doniphan that the Navajos were willing to talk. The two sides met at Ojo del Oso on November 21 with about 500 Navajos and about 700 American troops present.

The Navajos wondered why the Americans were so hostile toward them. After all, they were both fighting the Mexicans, and the Navajos had been fighting them longer. So why should the Americans interfere? Doniphan explained that the New Mexicans had surrendered and had become Americans, so Navajos who murdered and stole from New Mexicans were actually stealing from Americans. He asked the Navajos for peace and threatened them with the possibility of a long war if they did not agree.

The Navajos did not understand why Americans would conquer New Mexicans only to place them under American protection. But they did not want to fight the United States, so they accepted a treaty and exchanged gifts. For good measure, Doniphan then took three Navajo chiefs with him as guides when he visited the Zuni Indians. Doniphan and the Zunis were also able to come to an agreement.

As far as Doniphan was concerned, his job was done. He could put the Native American diversion behind him and get back to fighting the real war. Leaving Price in charge, he headed south toward the town of El Paso Del Norte, his next military objective.

In his haste to leave, Doniphan neglected to fully implement the terms of the treaty with the Indians. He made no arrangements for the exchange of prisoners or for the return of stolen property, and he failed to set up mechanisms by which the New Mexicans and Navajos could interact peacefully. He also did not bother to tell Charles Bent, the appointed civilian governor of New Mexico, about the terms of the treaty. In addition, a large portion of the Navajo tribe had not been present at the Ojo del Oso negotiations and did not agree to the treaty.

While it is difficult to understand Doniphan's sudden lack of judgment in dealing with the Indians, he appears to have had too much faith in American law and his own abilities as a diplomat. After all, his lawyerly diplomacy had worked in his past efforts in solving conflicts between American settlers. Unfortunately, because Doniphan lacked knowledge of Native American thought and customs, he was out of his depth when negotiating with them. His naive, Whig-like faith in the power of American law to quickly bring order and progress to the wilderness, combined with his misplaced trust in Sterling Price's capabilities to defend a meaningless treaty, doomed Doniphan's

Navajo effort to failure. In effect, he left behind multiple problems for Price that could not be cleaned up completely. It would take decades before the United States would finally quell the Navajo threat.

Doniphan assembled his forces, consisting of 856 soldiers and 300 to 400 traders, at Valverde on the east bank of the Rio Grande River not far from Socorro, which was at that time the main southernmost outpost in New Mexico. Their storied march was on again, and their first test would be crossing the ninety-mile Jornada del Muerto, or "Journey of the Dead." This terrible stretch of desert had only one watering hole, but braving the Jornada was less dangerous than following the Rio Grande, which wound through mountains that would leave the Missourians open to attack from Mexicans or Indians. Their passage was made especially difficult by winter weather, which blew snow and wind in their faces. To avoid detection, Doniphan decided not to use campfires, so the lack of warmth brought his troops even more misery.

It took Doniphan's men eight days to complete the journey across the Jornada to Dona Ana, where they paused for a day to regroup. Then the First Missouri Volunteers headed down the historic Camino Real, or "Kings Highway," south toward El Paso Del Norte, now Ciudad Juarez, where a large force of Mexicans was supposedly gathering to meet their advance.

Doniphan's army stopped early in the afternoon on Christmas Day 1846, at El Brazito, the "Little Arm" of the Rio Grande River in Mexico, about thirty miles north of El Paso. The defining moment in Doniphan's generalship, the Battle of El Brazito, would be forged a couple of hours later.

Not expecting any immediate action, Doniphan had placed a bare minimum of sentries around the camp to warn of an enemy attack. He was playing cards when scouts galloped excitedly into camp with the news that 1,200 Mexican soldiers in battle formation were headed their way. Doniphan threw down his cards in mock annoyance, telling the men they would have to resume their game later.

Arrayed in bright red uniforms, the Mexicans advanced—well tailored, well drilled, and well drawn up in neat marching lines. To display his contempt for the American invaders, their commander, Colonel Ponce De Leon, ordered an officer to ride out in front of the

Mexican War Volunteer at Brazito from John T. Hughes, *Doniphan's Expedition,* 1847. (State Historical Society of Missouri, Columbia.)

Americans and display a black flag on which were two skulls and cross-bones and the Spanish words *Libertad ó Muerte,* "Liberty or Death."

By proudly waving the black flag, the Mexicans let the Americans know that they would be given no quarter: the Mexicans would take no prisoners. Unless the Americans surrendered at once, they would have to face a fight to the death.

Doniphan sent an interpreter out to meet the Mexican officer. The officer demanded that Doniphan present himself, but the interpreter rejected the demand.

"We shall break your ranks and take him," the Mexican officer threatened.

"Come and take him," the American interpreter barked back. "Charge and be damned."

After a few more threats and American taunts in response, the Mexican galloped back to his own lines. While it may have stroked Colonel de Leon's ego, the dramatic gesture was a tactical mistake, wasting valuable time and taking away the element of surprise. It gave the Missourians time to organize a defense, and it steeled their resolve not to lose the battle.

Doniphan knew the Mexicans were equipped with old-fashioned and inaccurate British Brown Bess muskets with a range of fifty to sixty yards. To hit his men, the Mexicans would have to fire in groups to fill the air with shot.

Advancing toward the Missourians, the Mexican soldiers stopped and fired a volley from 400 yards away, and Doniphan decided to trick them. Each time the Mexicans fired a volley, he ordered some of his men to fall down as if they were hit. The Mexicans continued their march, stopping again to fire at 300 yards and again at 200 yards away, and with each volley, Doniphan ordered more of his men to fall to the ground.

At 100 yards, the Mexicans charged, confident that they had already crushed the American army. As the enemy closed in, Doniphan ordered his men to fire. About 200 Missouri riflemen stood up immediately and shot. The volley sent Mexican cavalry and infantry scattering in great confusion and wounded the Mexican commander. The Americans kept up a constant barrage of fire, and the disorganized and dispirited Mexicans began to run from the field.

An American cavalry charge captured a Mexican cannon, and the Mexican retreat quickly turned into a rout. In addition to the cannon, Doniphan's men collected other weaponry and many supplies, including wine, which made the Missourians' evening Christmas celebration a particularly joyous event.

Forty-three Mexicans were killed in the battle and 150 were wounded, according to American estimates, while Doniphan reported only seven wounded. The battle was over in less than an hour, and Doniphan had shown impressive leadership skills in defeating the much larger force of well-trained Mexicans with his ragged Missourians.

After the battle, Doniphan continued south and took El Paso Del Norte without resistance two days later. There he rested for a month and a half, taking the opportunity to resupply his army. He then decided to head farther south toward Chihuahua City, where his volunteers were supposed to join General John Wool's army. Although he had received no further communication since his original orders, going forward seemed like a better plan than staying too long where he was or going back to Santa Fe. Doniphan had been waiting for Meriwether Lewis Clark's artillery unit, which arrived on February 1,

1847. Clark's unit had been in Taos, New Mexico, helping Sterling Price quash a rebellion, in which Governor Charles Bent had been murdered. Doniphan now had more than 1,100 men with him including his Santa Fe traders.

At first, the Missourians marched down the Camino Real, but they learned the Mexicans had prepared impressive fortifications to meet them at the Sacramento River about fifteen miles north of Chihuahua. Doniphan's scouts occupied a mountaintop five miles from the Mexican lines and used field glasses to map the enemy position.

With input from his officers, Doniphan outlined a plan of attack. On the morning of February 8, he formed his nearly 400 wagons into four parallel columns about thirty feet apart. He placed Clark's artillery between the two middle wagon columns, and positioned the rest of his infantry equally split between spaces inside the wagon columns. He put three companies of cavalry in front.

The enemy blocked the road to Chihuahua with a line of trenches and circular redoubts, or protective towers, at intervals of 300 to 500 yards that could spray the Missourians with shot if they tried a frontal charge. Studying the Mexican defenses, Doniphan's scouts found a passage to the left of the Mexican line that would allow his forces to maneuver around the enemy trenches.

As he marched toward the Mexican lines, about two miles away, Doniphan ordered his men to march forty-five degrees to the right onto a plateau that allowed them to avoid the Mexican guns and outflank the Mexicans on their left wing. To mask the maneuver, Doniphan sent his cavalry forward to momentarily distract the Mexicans.

The Mexican commander, Major General Jose A. Heredia, realized the implications of Doniphan's maneuver and turned his troops to face the Americans on the plateau. About 1,000 Mexican cavalry charged the advancing Americans, but they were beaten back by Clark's artillery. Nestled between the wagon columns, the guns had been hidden from Mexican view.

The artillery duel lasted for nearly an hour; the Mexican shots often fell short because their gunpowder did not throw their cannonballs with enough velocity. The Americans, however, were hitting their mark, slowly reducing the Mexican fortifications to rubble and demoralizing the defenders.

According to Roger Launius, while Doniphan sat calmly in his saddle, whittling a stick, a pose that would "reassure his men and frustrate his enemy," he ordered a charge. One infantry battalion surged forward on the right and the other on the left, and Clark's artillery, supported by cavalry, moved forward in the center.

The Americans now faced the fury of the Mexican cannons. One cavalry charge against a gun battery succeeded for a moment, but the mounted troops fell back when a portion of the unit mistakenly heard an order to halt. They regrouped and recaptured the battery.

The infantry on the right of the American line, fighting hand-to-hand, captured three batteries, while its defenders turned and ran. Meanwhile, the Missourians on the left of the line charged the Mexican cavalry and then flanked and routed the Mexican infantry from their redoubts.

The remaining Mexicans retreated to the Sacramento River hills and prepared to make a last stand with their artillery. While Clark's artillery shelled and blasted the Mexican forces with howitzers, an American cavalry unit surrounded and surprised the enemy by attacking their rear. The Mexicans were forced to surrender.

The battle, which lasted about three hours, was a complete victory for the Missourians. There were almost 700 Mexicans killed, wounded, or captured. On the American side, there were only two casualties and six wounded.

The battles of El Brazito and Sacramento cemented Doniphan's place as a war hero alongside other military leaders of the Mexican War, such as Zachary Taylor. Doniphan was seen as the epitome of the American citizen soldier.

Governor Angel Trias fled southward, and Doniphan occupied Chihuahua City on March 1. The citizens were not friendly to the Americans, having much closer ties to Mexico City than the New Mexicans did, and Doniphan found it necessary to declare martial law. When he got news of the decisive victory at the Battle of Buena Vista, and General Winfield Scott's landing at Vera Cruz and subsequent march on Mexico City, Doniphan knew the war would end soon. After nearly two months in Chihuahua, Doniphan received orders to join General Taylor's army at Saltillo, about 600 miles away. It was time to push eastward to join Generals Taylor and Wool.

After another arduous journey, Doniphan met General Wool's forces on May 21. Astonished at their ragged appearance, Wool reviewed the men and listened to a report of their accomplishments. The Missourians marched the rest of the way to Monterrey to meet with General Taylor's forces and then on to the coast, where they arranged for transport home.

Doniphan and his Missourians returned to a hero's welcome, arriving in New Orleans in June for the trip up the Mississippi. When they reached St. Louis, the festivities were especially brilliant. Doniphan then headed home to his wife and law practice. He would have some traveling and speech making to do as well.

The Whig Party wanted him to run for governor or for U.S. senator, but he declined. In Mexico, he had been ill, and his health was never the same. His wife also was in poor health and would later suffer a stroke. He had not seen her in a year, and he needed to rebuild his law practice. In addition, during the 1850s, Doniphan and his wife lost both of their sons in freak accidents, putting a heavy emotional burden on them. His eldest son accidentally took poison, and his youngest drowned while swimming.

If he had jumped immediately into the political fray upon his return from Mexico, we might know Doniphan today as an ex-senator or ex-governor. Of course, that is assuming that his popularity as a war hero could have overcome his affiliation with the Whig Party, which rarely held much power in Missouri, where the main contest was often between different factions of Democrats.

In the end, Doniphan's inability to gauge new political realities may have been his undoing. While useful in antebellum Missouri, both his Whig Party affiliation and his devoted pursuit of compromise and consensus would run aground over the question of slavery as the border war with Kansas developed into a full-scale rebellion.

The annexation of Texas and the accession of new lands in the Southwest accelerated the conflict over the expansion of slavery. Many predicted that the institution would eventually wither and die, but it did not.

The Missouri Compromise of 1820 that allowed Missouri to gain statehood in 1821 gave way to the Kansas-Nebraska Act of 1854, and each new state was given the right to decide for itself whether to

This George Caleb Bingham portrait of Elizabeth Jane Thornton Doniphan, *ca.* 1850, was painted after Doniphan's return from the Mexican War. Bingham also painted portraits of Doniphan and of the Doniphans' two sons, John Thornton and William Alexander Jr. Art historians believe the portraits of the sons were painted after their deaths. (State Historical Society of Missouri, Columbia.)

be a slave or a free state. Settlers from Missouri and from northern states poured into Kansas, where, as the situation evolved, both proslavery and antislavery factions set up rival territorial governments with separate constitutions. Missouri bushwhackers and Kansas Jayhawkers raided each other's farms. Both groups lynched opponents and burned down homesteads.

With violence increasing and Civil War imminent, Doniphan did his best to help forge a compromise to save his beloved South and the Union. According to Launius, he opposed secession, never accepting the states' rights argument, and spoke against it forcefully in Liberty, Jefferson City, and Washington. He was a delegate to the state convention called to study the secession question in Jefferson City and represented Missouri in the Peace Conference called by the Virginia legislature in February 1861.

But it was not a time for compromisers. In this war, every man had to choose a side. Doniphan tried to walk a middle course, to be a peacemaker, and by doing so, he lost the respect of a populace polarized by a war in which men were forced to take up arms against their friends and relatives.

He had proven to be a good peacemaker during the Mormon War, but that was a different conflict. Some Missourians had sympathy for the Mormons. But this time around, peacemakers were out of style, and the time for peacemaking was past.

Doniphan believed in the Union and would not turn against it. But he also believed in slavery and the Old South. It horrified him that his country would choose to go through the same kind of political strife the people of Mexico had endured in their civil war when all that was called for was a little sanity and compromise. He sincerely thought that a middle way could be forged to preserve both the institution of slavery and the Union. He tried to support gradual emancipation, but it was too late for compromise on the slavery issue.

Missouri general M. Jeff Thompson was at the April 23, 1861, mass meeting held in Liberty when Doniphan, "of Mexican War celebrity," spoke before the assembly. "His words were rich in their praise of the South and condemnation of the aggressive Spirit of abolitionism. . . . He made a powerful appeal to the people to stand by their Southern brethren," wrote Thompson in his memoirs. After Doniphan's fiery speech, Thompson was astounded at the "submissive spirit" and "devotion to the Union" offered in the resolutions approved later and was further amazed when "General Doniphan, who had spoken with so much fire, quietly folded the comforts of his home around him, and has been an idle spectator . . . while every vestige of his honor has been swept from him."

The resolutions adopted in Liberty "applauded Gov. Jackson's refusal to furnish troops to the federal government, called for an immediate recognition of the Confederacy—with an offensive-

Alexander William Doniphan. This portrait of Doniphan is from the *United States Biographical Dictionary,* Missouri, published in 1878. His last years were saddened by the deaths of his sons and his wife. (State Historical Society of Missouri, Columbia.)

defensive alliance, and called on Missouri to remain neutral as long as possible," according to John Glendower Westover. Governor Jackson offered Doniphan a generalship in the militia, which he declined.

Doniphan was unable to condemn slavery, but, at the same time, he was unwilling to rebel against his country, which meant that neither side could count on him. In an era of strong feelings, Doniphan remained neutral and became politically irrelevant. By not choosing a side, Doniphan saw his political career fade.

Doniphan's wife died in 1873. He lived until 1887 in a boarding house in Richmond, sometimes granting interviews to newspapers, but financially troubled and often lonely. In early 1887, the U.S. Congress had passed the Mexican War Pension Act, and three months before his death on August 8, 1887, the pension office approved his claim for a land grant and a military pension.

At his funeral Doniphan's pallbearers were all members of his Mexican regiment and the eulogies from those who remembered him spoke of his great deeds on the road to Chihuahua.

For more reading

"Alexander William Doniphan: Missouri's Forgotten Leader," essay by Roger D. Launius, in *Missouri Folk Heroes of the 19th Century*, edited by F. Mark McKiernan and Roger Launius (Independence, Mo.: Herald Publishing House, 1989).

Alexander William Doniphan: Portrait of a Missouri Moderate, by Roger D. Launius (Columbia: University of Missouri Press, 1997), paints an intriguing picture of Doniphan as a great compromiser.

Doniphan's Epic March: The First Missouri Volunteers in the Mexican War, by Joseph G. Dawson (Lawrence: University Press of Kansas, 1999), is a good account of Doniphan's expedition into New Mexico and Mexico during the Mexican War, but it barely touches on other aspects of Doniphan's life.

The 1838 Mormon War in Missouri, by Stephen C. LeSueur (Columbia: University of Missouri Press, 1987), is a readable and well-documented study that provides detailed information about the conflict in Missouri.

3

Sterling Price

Born in Virginia in 1809, Sterling Price was descended from Welsh immigrants who were early settlers in the Jamestown Colony. He arrived in Missouri in 1831 at the age of 22 and established a farm near Keytesville in Chariton County.

Within two years, he married a very eligible young woman named Martha Head, and within another two years, they had the first of seven children, five of whom lived to adulthood. Price quickly became a country squire at his beloved manor, which he named "Val Verde."

He soon became prominent in the Boonslick region, an amorphous collection of towns and counties along the Missouri River in central Missouri that got its name from a salt operation Daniel Boone's sons established in the early 1800s near the present town of Boonville. In addition to his farming activities, Price opened a general store in Keytesville and speculated in real estate. He also joined the Chariton County militia, which elected him colonel, and in 1838 his neighbors elected him to the state legislature.

Price believed wholeheartedly in the southern way of life as he saw it—a peaceful, agrarian, and orderly society run by honorable, wealthy country gentleman planters and supported by slave labor—and he and others lived it in Missouri. It was a Jeffersonian dream, almost utopian for the elite gentlemen who ran things. For the workers laboring for the benefit of a master, it was less of a dream and more of a nightmare.

Sterling Price served in the Missouri General Assembly, in the U.S. House of Representatives, and as commander of the Second Missouri Volunteers in the Mexican War before his election as the eleventh governor of Missouri in 1852. (Missouri State Archives.)

Price was a Democrat and a member of a political group known as the Boonslick Democracy, which supported the principles of President Andrew Jackson that dominated Missouri politics before the Civil War. The Boonslick Democrats believed that individual and local rights should prevail over a strong federal government. They also thought that political leaders should come from the social elite—men like themselves—proud southerners, slaveholders, planters, and merchants.

This preference for local sovereignty would directly affect the states' rights debate that would lead to the Civil War, and Price played a prominent role in early phases of Missouri's secession crisis. Late in the Civil War, he would become famous for leading a desperate raid

Martha Head Price, like her husband a native of Virginia, managed the 400-acre farm in Chariton County and took care of four young children while General Price was in Mexico. She and one of the children were ill during his campaign for governor, but she moved to Jefferson City for the inaugural ceremonies. The Price's seventh child, a son, was born in the governor's residence a month before the term ended. (Reprinted from *Women of the Mansion, Missouri, 1821–1936,* by Eleanora G. Park and Kate S. Morrow. Courtesy of the State Historical Society of Missouri, Columbia.)

into Missouri aimed at returning his beloved state to the southern fold.

Although they were members of different political parties, Price had much in common with Alexander W. Doniphan. They were both citizen soldiers, and, although Price did not become a lawyer, both were trained in the law.

Like Doniphan, and others of their generation, Price eventually had to come to grips with his position on slavery. He came to believe that slavery was evil, but he hated abolitionists and antislavery Jayhawkers from Kansas, and he abhorred the federal government's willingness to push his state into a war it did not want. Although Doniphan chose to remain neutral during the Civil War, Price turned to the Confederacy because of his strong belief in states' rights, splitting with the Union when the federal government began to use force against Missouri.

When Price won a second term in the legislature in 1840, the House unanimously elected him Speaker. Like Doniphan, he had become heavily involved in the Mormon War of 1838 and had gained much political prestige from his involvement, but he had viewed the issue differently. Although he thought many of the accusations against the Mormons were unfounded, he joined other leading Chariton County citizens in asking Governor Lilburn Boggs to call out the militia. Price commanded the Chariton County militia, within the division answering to General John B. Clark, to whom Governor Boggs had given the infamous Extermination Order to kill or drive the Mormons from Missouri. Clark ordered Price to take control of the captured Mormon leaders being sent to Independence for a civil trial after Doniphan's public protest caused General Lucas to reverse his decision to execute them.

Price supported the state militia's treatment of the Mormons. As far as he was concerned, he had done his patriotic duty in helping to expel them, protecting Missouri against a fanatical sect that planned to subvert the social and political order of his state and his beloved southern way of life. In 1844, after his involvement in the Mormon War, at the age of thirty-five, he was elected to the U.S. House of Representatives, and his political career appeared to be moving forward quickly. Although he did not accomplish much in Washington, he performed his duties diligently. He introduced only two bills, one for a study of a mail route between Quincy, Illinois, and St. Joseph, and the second for Missourians to be repaid for horses they lost during the Seminole campaigns in Florida.

Two years later, the nominating convention of his district decided to choose someone else to run for his seat in the House. With the Mexican War brewing, he resigned to take a militia command that was similar to Doniphan's. Price's appointment was gained through the influence of his benefactor, Senator Thomas Hart Benton. Doniphan commanded the First Missouri Volunteers, and Price would command the Second.

It would prove to be a pattern. Wherever Doniphan went, Price followed, and he often had to solve some problem left behind by Doniphan. Price's Second Missouri Volunteers occupied Santa Fe after Doniphan headed south and would later occupy Chihuahua after Doniphan's group headed home. After Doniphan and his men left New Mexico, Price had to suppress a revolt during which the territorial governor was assassinated. He received a promotion to brigadier general for his role in effectively stopping the Taos Rebellion and went on to stop similar insurrections in El Paso Del Norte and Chihuahua.

While Price was perhaps more politically astute than Doniphan, he was also extremely stubborn and was considered particularly vain about his military skills. Although Price and Doniphan's commander, General Stephen Watts Kearny, had requested that the Second regiment consist primarily of infantry, Price preferred leading cavalry troops, so he ignored Kearny's request and raised mounted troops instead. As biographer Robert Shalhope said, Price "was already evincing a certain vanity regarding his own judgment that would cause him problems throughout his military career."

Vanity aside, Price had a good ear for popular sentiment. He clamped down on troop discipline in Santa Fe, a necessary action that helped ease tensions with the New Mexican population. Discipline had grown lax under Doniphan, who had won his command by promising very little of it, a situation that generated resentment among the civilians. When Doniphan left Santa Fe to go after the Navajos, Price took command in the town and instituted regular military drills, but he was not entirely successful in maintaining order. After several weeks, the troops fell back into their old habits again.

In addition, according to Shalhope, many of Price's officers resented his political appointment and openly ridiculed his attempts to impose further discipline. In their view, Price had received his command not because of his military prowess but because of his political connections, and they believed that he did not know what he was doing. Some hoped he would fail in his pursuit of military glory.

His military prowess was tested during the Taos Rebellion, which broke out on January 18, 1847. New Mexican rebels shot Governor Charles Bent and tortured or killed other officials. An American attorney was forced to strip and walk naked through the streets while Indians shot him full of arrows. He was then scalped alive and killed. The rebellion quickly spread to several other New Mexico towns.

Five days later, Price left Santa Fe with 350 men, mostly dismounted, and four howitzers. The Mexican rebels occupied three houses in the town of Canada and the heights above the village. Price positioned his artillery so that his guns could bombard the Mexican positions. Then his men charged the rebel positions, defeating them soundly. The rebels lost thirty-six men, while the Americans only lost two.

Price then moved toward the village of El Embudo, where his troops scattered a rebel force before pushing through deep snow to Taos, where the enemy was barricaded in a pueblo complex with thick adobe walls. Inside the walls of the complex were a large church to the northwest and other tall buildings from which the rebels could fire down upon the Missourians. Price ordered an artillery barrage, but then retreated for the night when his men ran out of ammunition.

The next day, Price decided that taking the church was the top priority. After firing his howitzers at the walls for two hours with little effect, he ordered troops to charge to the north and the west walls of the fortress. He had noticed that there was a space between the church and outer wall that would protect his men from the enemy fire. Once at the fortress wall, his men chopped a hole through the adobe with axes. One group charged inside the hole but was beaten back by the enemy. Another group lobbed explosives through the hole, then slowly enlarged it into a big gap with artillery fire.

Under the cover of the gun smoke, the Missourians stormed the church. Once they had taken it, they charged the village. The Mexicans tried to escape, but Price had placed a regiment of Missourians in their path to stop them. In revenge for the Taos massacre, the Missourians gave very little quarter to the retreating Mexicans.

Price had proved himself. It was a crushing defeat for the Mexican rebels. He then presided over a reign of terror reminiscent of the French Revolution, during which one rebel a day was hung for fifteen days straight by an American court. While bloody, the tactic kept New Mexico quiet for the rest of the war. Impartiality was not the order of the day for the court. The son of the inquiry's presiding officer had been killed at Taos, the foreman of the jury was the dead governor's brother, and the rest of the jury was composed of relatives and friends of the dead Americans.

The prosecutor was Attorney General Frank P. Blair, who later became one of Price's main adversaries in state government and during Missouri's secession crisis. Blair accused the rebels of treason because General Kearny had declared New Mexico to be American territory. In a move reminiscent of Doniphan's refusal to execute the

Mormons, however, Price pardoned one of the rebel leaders with the permission of Secretary of State James Buchanan. When Blair objected, Price had him arrested. Blair resigned, and the resulting feud between the two continued for years, culminating in the secession crisis at the beginning of the Civil War.

Blair was not Price's only political enemy. A year before the Blair incident, Price had quarreled with Jefferson Davis. Davis wanted to switch commands with Price so that he would not have to serve under his father-in-law, Zachary Taylor, whom he disliked. Price refused his request. To add to Davis's resentment, Price then received a promotion to brigadier general for his role in stopping the Taos Rebellion. Davis, on the other hand, was not promoted for his heroism at the Battle of Buena Vista. Davis never forgot either incident and was highly resentful of Price. Subsequently, during the Civil War, when Davis became president of the Confederacy, he often passed Price over for promotions in the Confederate army.

The incident with Davis, and Price's appointment through his political connections, led to the perception that Price was a politician's general, a label he would never completely overcome. No matter what he accomplished in civilian or military life, he would have to battle the accusation that his actions were based more on political expediency and a desire for personal glory than on military necessity.

But Price's Mexican War adventures were not finished. After a trip home for a couple of months, he returned to New Mexico in January 1848 with a small force of dragoons, arriving in Santa Fe almost a year after the Taos Rebellion to command the Third Missouri and First Illinois Volunteer regiments. Once again, it was up to Price to instill military discipline in a force of raw recruits, who were more in the mood to party and pillage than to train. In late February 1848, he reported rumors that Mexican troops were gathering again in Chihuahua and El Paso after Doniphan's forces had left, and he decided to march southward, ignoring War Department orders to remain in his own district. He had wanted to make such an incursion for some time, and now he had his chance.

When Price and his men reached El Paso, they discovered that the rumors of an attack on the city had been false, and they headed farther south in search of enemy forces to engage. On March 5, north of Chihuahua, a messenger from Governor Angel Trias met with Price, protesting this new U.S. invasion and saying the Mexican government had already signed a peace treaty on February 2, 1848. Price did not take the governor at his word and occupied Chihuahua City after a group of Americans from Chihuahua told him the Mexican army had left the city.

Price then cornered the Mexican army at the town of Santa Cruz de Rosales and sent a messenger under a flag of truce to seek their surrender. Trias spoke to Price, again telling him that a peace treaty had been signed. Price decided to besiege the town and await confirmation.

After waiting for a week without word, on March 16, 1848 Price decided to attack Santa Cruz de Rosales. The artillery opened fire from several directions at once, and the Missourians charged. Advancing along the rooftops and through the streets in fierce hand-to-hand combat, they threw hand grenades made from howitzer shells. Ducking into Mexican homes to avoid snipers, the Missourians also had to dodge Mexican grenades, many of which the Missourians hurled back at the enemy.

Eventually, Price's men reached the plaza at the center of town. The Mexicans had taken shelter in a church but surrendered as the Americans began to storm it. Unfortunately, some of the attacking Missourians did not get the message that the hostilities had ended, and many Mexicans were killed while expecting quarter.

With the town secured, on March 16, cleanup of the bodies commenced. Only four Americans had been killed and only nineteen had been wounded, but about two hundred Mexicans had died. After the city was taken, Price served as the provincial military governor until July 1848, when the Missourians headed home.

Although later critics would question the necessity of Price's attack on Santa Cruz de Rosales, it had been a successful military campaign, and it rivaled any of Doniphan's military victories. Mexico City had fallen six months before his Chihuahua campaign, while the Treaty of Guadelupe Hidalgo had been signed a month before, and ratified six days prior to, his attack on Santa Cruz de Rosales. Price did not have confirmation of these facts at the time he decided to attack, but he also disregarded last-minute orders from his superiors to stop the campaign. Nevertheless, when he returned from the Mexican War, he was hailed as a hero and elected governor of Missouri in 1852. Price served one term, from 1853 to 1857. At that time, according to the Missouri state constitution, governors could serve only one term.

As governor, Price saw his role as something of a manager of the state. He would simply pass judgment on acts of the legislature and did not pursue any initiatives of his own. Although he could claim no major accomplishments, his term went well and his political fortunes continued to rise. As Price's term ended, storm clouds were brewing in the state. A political split had occurred in the 1850s between those Democrats who supported and those who opposed former longtime senator Thomas Hart Benton. To assure his election to the governor's office, Price had decided he would no longer support Benton, who had been his benefactor but had lost his senate seat in 1851. When the Missouri legislature nominated Price for U.S. senator in 1857, Frank Blair, Price's Mexican War nemesis and a leading Bentonite, publicly accused Price of betraying his mentor.

This political feuding intensified hostilities already inflamed by the atrocities of the border war taking place in western Missouri. A few years later, in 1860, Price would serve as president of the state convention studying the issue of Missouri's secession from the Union. The convention decided that Missouri should not secede, but its members opposed any federal coercion to keep the state in the Union.

Missouri's future was at stake, and former governor Price stood at the center of the events that resulted in a long and bitter Civil War in Missouri. While General William Selby Harney, commander of the Department of the West in St. Louis, was in Washington defending himself against charges that he was too sympathetic to the South, his pro-Union subordinate Captain Nathaniel Lyon and Unionist Frank Blair had secretly mustered regiments of Home Guards, composed primarily of German immigrants, and were ready to capture the state militia encamped in the city. Daniel M. Frost, commander of the St. Louis district, had urged Governor Jackson to call up the militia, and he had hoped to establish his encampment, named for the governor, on a site overlooking the St. Louis Arsenal. Since Lyon's troops had already occupied this site, he set up Camp Jackson at Lindell Grove at the west edge of the city.

Governor Jackson had requested arms from Confederate president Jefferson Davis, and Davis sent "two 12-pound howitzers and two thirty-two pound siege guns, 500 muskets, and a large amount of ammunition" to Camp Jackson from the arsenal in Baton Rouge, according to Blair biographer William E. Parrish. When Lyon and Blair surrounded Camp Jackson, Frost surrendered his militia under protest but without incident. As the Home Guards marched the prisoners toward the arsenal, however, a crowd that had gathered started taunting and throwing rocks at Lyon's men. Someone in the crowd fired on the troops, and the Home Guards returned fire. Twenty-eight civilians died, including women and children.

Although those captured were paroled the next day, the Camp Jackson Affair, as it came to be known, represented exactly the kind of federal coercion Price did not support. It would soon drive him, along with many of his fellow Missourians, to join the Confederacy.

When Harney returned, he worked out a compromise with Price on May 21 to keep the peace, but Congressman Frank Blair, working with Lyon, convinced President Lincoln to recall Harney to Washington and to put Lyon in charge. Lyon and Blair then met with Price and Governor Jackson on June 11, 1861, to see if they could reach an accord. After listening to Price and Jackson for a few minutes, Lyon stood and, according to a newspaper at the time, told the group, "Better that the blood of every man, woman, and child within the limits of the State should flow than that she should defy the federal government." Then he strode out of the room, leaving Blair to make a less combative exit.

In a different version of the incident in his 1886 book, Price associate Colonel Thomas Snead quoted Lyon as saying, "I would see you, and you, and you, and you, and you, and every man, woman and child in the State dead and buried." Whichever version is closest to the truth, the different accounts show the deep distrust and differing perspectives held by both sides.

Lyon's outburst meant war. Price and Jackson headed quickly to Jefferson City by train, burning the railroad bridges and cutting the telegraph wires behind them to slow down any advance by Lyon's Union troops. Lyon's force followed soon after, by boat, and occupied the state capital after an amphibious assault at Jefferson

Southern morale rose after the battle of Wilson's Creek in Southwest Missouri. Although Price's militia was "badly organized, badly armed, and almost entirely out of ammunition" in the summer of 1861, he agreed to join Confederate general Ben McCulloch in a joint movement against Lyon. But rain and wet ammunition delayed the Confederate march on Springfield, and Lyon attacked their encampment at Wilson's Creek on August 10, 1861. Price was wounded, and Lyon lost his life. (State Historical Society of Missouri, Columbia.)

Landing. Before Lyon's troops reached the city, the governor and other state officials fled the capital, taking the state seal with them.

Governor Jackson called on the state militia to assemble under Price's command. He ordered his nephew, John S. Marmaduke, to stop Lyon at Boonville with a state militia force. The skirmish went so badly for the poorly trained and ill-equipped state troops that the encounter became known as the "Boonville Races" because the state force ran away from the enemy. Marmaduke resigned from the state militia and went to Virginia to join the Confederacy. After members of the Missouri state convention, meeting in Jefferson City, voted to elect a provisional governor in his place on July 22, Jackson still tried to rally support for secession, and on August 5, in New Madrid, he issued a "Proclamation of Independence," declaring Missouri an independent state. Soon after, however, he took his family and his slaves from his Saline County home and went south, eventually forming a government in exile in Marshall, Texas. Missouri thereby gained a star on the Confederate flag even though it remained in the Union.

Price, who had been ill at his home in Keytesville when Lyon occupied Jefferson City, led his hastily organized army of state troops to southwest Missouri after Marmaduke's defeat at Boonville. The raw recruits, many without firearms, needed training to face the better-prepared and better-equipped federal forces. Lyon pursued him with 6,000 men and decided to attack Price's 12,000-man army on August 10, 1861, at Wilson's Creek near Springfield. Lyon had requested reinforcements from the new commanding general of Union forces in the West, General John C. Frémont, who was head-quartered in St. Louis. Frémont denied Lyon's request and advised him to retreat to Rolla if he did not think he could win the battle. To the dismay of most of his staff, Lyon instead decided to follow a strategy proposed by Colonel Franz Sigel, the leader of the "Dutch Volunteers," an independent brigade made up mainly of German immigrants. Lyon thought he might surprise Price, even though Price's force was considerably larger, but while leading a charge up Bloody Hill, Lyon was killed and his troops were defeated.

Price then headed north again with 7,000 men, a force that grew to at least 10,000 as he picked up recruits. On September 18, at Lexington, he surrounded and bombarded Colonel James A. Mulligan's 27,000 Union troops who had fortified themselves on the grounds of the Masonic College on the northern end of town. Using wet hemp bales taken from a warehouse for protection—the Union artillery could not penetrate the dense bales—Price slowly moved his men east toward the Union lines and defeated Mulligan's forces on the third day of the siege. Eventually, lacking water and officers who weren't wounded, Mulligan was forced to surrender. The Lexington victory brought Price five artillery pieces, 3,000 rifles, and 750 horses; he also returned $900,000 that had been looted from the local bank. But he and his men were soon forced by the approach of General John C. Frémont's troops to retreat to southwest Missouri.

Price called for more Missouri volunteers, but he did not get the response he had hoped for. He quarreled with General Benjamin

Price's men admired his bravery and often spoke of the compassion he showed for those in his command. A song about the Confederate loss in the battle at Pea Ridge on March 26, 1862, which survived in the Ozarks for more than a century, documents Price's grief at the loss his men suffered: "Cap' Price came riding up the line / His horse was in a pace / And as he gave the word 'retreat'/ The tears rolled down his face." General Earl Van Dorn praised the Missourians in his report: "I have never seen better troops than these Missouri troops or more gallant leaders than General Price and his officers." (Missouri State Archives.)

McCulloch, the Confederate commander in the West, for not following up the Missouri victories with an attack on St. Louis. With larger Union forces pursuing him, Price had to retreat into Arkansas. There, under the command of Confederate general Earl Van Dorn, Price and McCulloch fought Union general Samuel Curtis at the Battle of Pea Ridge in northern Arkansas. While Price's Missourians fought valiantly, standing firm when veteran regulars under the other Confederate generals faltered, it was not enough to stave off defeat.

Price's men covered the withdrawal of Van Dorn's army, whose plans of a possible attack on Missouri had been thwarted by the loss.

After Missouri officially joined the Confederacy on November 18, 1861, President Davis made Price a major general in the Confederate army and transferred him to Tennessee. Now under the command of General P. G. T. Beauregard, Price fought in several engagements, tangling in Mississippi with Grant at Iuka and with William Rosecrans at Corinth. Deciding to focus on the eastern states, Davis chose to write Missouri off, letting the state fall to the Union, much to Price's dismay.

Price kept asking for a chance to invade Missouri, and he decided to plead his case with Davis in Richmond, Virginia, the capital of the Confederacy. Arriving there, he was received with great fanfare as a hero for his "victory at Lexington and courage at Pea Ridge," according to biographer Albert Castel. The *Daily Richmond Whig* announced on June 16, 1862, that "the Washington of the West is now in Richmond—All Hail!"

When Price went in person to ask for a command west of the Mississippi, Davis refused. After an argument, Price threatened to resign and to raise his own army without help from the Confederacy. He returned to his hotel, prepared his resignation, and sent it to Davis, who returned it to Price the next day. Then, snubbing Price, Davis gave the western command in Arkansas to a close personal friend, Theophilus Holmes, and transferred Price to serve under Holmes's command.

During his time east of the Mississippi, Price's son Edwin returned home to seek a pardon for his part in the rebellion, a pardon he eventually received from President Lincoln. Price was angered by his son's action, but he could not stop him from going back to his family. With it relatively well known that Price was not happy with Jefferson Davis and the Confederate government's unwillingness to let him lead an invasion of Missouri, rumors began to circulate that his son's turncoat status might be a prelude to his own possible switch of allegiance to the Union side. Some even thought Price might quit the Confederacy and lead a new rebellion of northern midwestern states that would form their own government.

When Holmes fell ill, Price took over the western army and in 1864 decided to invade Missouri. Price believed that thousands of young men would answer his call and come to the aid of the Confederacy. Much like Pickett's charge at Gettysburg, Price's raid, possibly because it came so late in the war, would become a turning point that would break the back of the Southern cause west of the Mississippi.

On September 19, 1864, Price advanced into southeast Missouri leading an army of three divisions headed by James Fagan, John S. Marmaduke, and Joseph Shelby. Thomas Reynolds, who had become governor-in-exile after the death of Governor Jackson, and other politicians accompanied the Confederate invaders, hoping to install Reynold's government in Jefferson City. General M. Jeff Thompson, the "Confederate Swamp Fox," who had recently been released from prison, also joined Price's raid, even though he lacked a command. Later, when Colonel David Shanks was killed, Thompson took command of his unit.

Price's primary objective was to take St. Louis, but, on the advice of Fagan and Marmaduke, he decided to first attack a small Union force at Pilot Knob. The Union soldiers withstood charge after charge from Price's army and suffered immense losses, but so did Price's men. Commanding the fort at Pilot Knob was Kansas general Thomas Ewing, whose famous Order Number 11 issued in 1863 had forced families in western Missouri border counties to evacuate their homes. He did not want to be captured, and his Union forces abandoned the fort in the middle of the night. When Price's Confederates took the fort the next day, they technically won the battle, but it was an empty victory. He had lost so many men that it crippled his ability to push toward his major objective of taking St. Louis, and it would later prevent him from capturing Jefferson City.

Throughout the march, Price failed to stop his men from pillaging and retaliating against Union officers and soldiers accused of committing atrocities against southern sympathizers. His men freely lynched and shot the Union troops they had captured. These were the same sort of tactics used by irregular cutthroats on both sides of the conflict, such as bushwhackers William Quantrill and "Bloody Bill" Anderson, and Kansas Jayhawker Charles Jennison, marauding across Missouri. But one of the main goals of Price's raid was to recruit men to fight for the Confederate cause, and these revenge lynchings and killings made even southern sympathizers think twice about joining Price's army.

Price threatened St. Louis, but he did not dare to attack with his depleted force. As he turned west, Marmaduke's division made a foray into Hermann, a known pro-Union stronghold, destroying property and confiscating much-needed supplies. The German writer, Gert Goebel, a resident of Franklin County, wrote: "General Price and Shelby followed the old highway to Jefferson City but the pack of thieves which accompanied the army spread out several miles to the right and the left robbing and plundering."

Price also decided that Jefferson City was too heavily fortified for an attack, and he continued his march farther west. Often ailing, Price spent much of the trek across Missouri in a carriage. Groups of men led by Quantrill, Anderson, and George Todd met with him in Boonville in mid-October 1864. Price ordered them to destroy the Northern Missouri and the Hannibal-St. Louis railroads. Quantrill decided the mission was bound to fail. Leaving George Todd in command of those guerrillas who wished to remain with Price, Quantrill left the state with a small force. The Missouri militia killed Anderson in Ray County in October and found Price's orders on his body. Todd would also die that month while battling Union troops near Independence. Union rangers fatally wounded Quantrill the next year in Kentucky.

As Price's army moved through central Missouri, he sent John B. Clark's brigade, supported by Shelby and his brigade, to raid Glasgow in Howard County, and Jeff Thompson captured Sedalia in Pettis County, forcing the federal militia to surrender. Thompson claimed in his memoirs that he managed to prevent pillaging by threatening men who took property from civilians with his sword.

Price's men encountered Union troops east of Independence and fought a major battle to take the town, pushing the Union forces westward to the Big Blue River. Price's westward march was stopped at Westport, where his forces were soundly defeated by Price's old Arkansas nemesis, General Samuel R. Curtis, who was now the Union commander in Kansas. Curtis now joined forces with General Alfred S. Pleasanton, whose troops had been following Price's army since his aborted raid on Jefferson City, to spring a trap on Price's army.

On October 22, 1864, Price's army crossed the Big Blue River, east of the towns of Kansas City and Westport, and headed west to crush Curtis. After a short evening skirmish, Curtis's forces retreated to earthworks around Kansas City. Price's men were positioned in a line, starting on the high ground south of Brush Creek and heading eastward across the Wornall Road all the way to the Big Blue. Price planned for his forces to hold General Pleasonton's men to the east while they first defeated General Curtis's forces to the north.

Curtis had 15,000 men, and Pleasonton had 6,500 cavalrymen. Price had only 9,000 soldiers, but he was confident that he could win. After all, he and Doniphan had faced similar odds in Mexico.

But that was in a different era against a different foe. The next morning, Pleasonton's forces attacked from the east, knocking General Marmaduke's battalion from Independence and the heights on the west bank of the Big Blue River, a position that Price had thought virtually impossible to take. Meanwhile, Curtis's men marched southward from Westport to Brush Creek. Wading across it, they took cover in the trees on the south bank, with an artillery unit set up behind them, to wait for Price's army.

They didn't have long to wait. General Shelby led a Confederate cavalry attack northward against Curtis's position. Curtis called for his reserves, and the Union troops slowly beat back Shelby's men. At the same time, Pleasanton's artillery wreaked havoc on Marmaduke's soldiers to the east. At noon, Pleasonton's troops charged over the Big Blue heights, the position they had taken earlier in the day, pushing hard on Price's right flank.

Price's center, under General Fagan, was now cut off from Shelby's men on the left, while at the same time Price's right wing under Marmaduke was collapsing under Pleasonton's blistering attack. Fagan's and Marmaduke's lines collapsed, and their forces began retreating at full speed, leaving Shelby alone to face the onslaught of Curtis. Shelby held his position valiantly, retreating only at sunset, but having lost more than 800 men.

The remnants of Price's Confederate army reassembled at Marais des Cygnes and continued retreating under heavy attack from the Union cavalry. Marmaduke, who was in the rear guard, was captured along with several hundred other Confederate soldiers. Price's grand invasion was over.

Price's battered army retreated all the way to Texas with the Union army on its heels. They stayed in Texas for several months, the officers blaming each other for the failure of the expedition. As time wore on, Price found himself having to defend his actions against accusations of incompetence in military hearings.

Before these hearings could be concluded, Robert E. Lee surrendered to Ulysses S. Grant at Appomattox, and it was clear that the Confederacy was dying. The Confederate generals in Texas decided to fight on in the west, but Price's army quickly disintegrated. The men were tired and wanted to go home.

Price fled to Mexico with some of his men, where he tried to re-create his plantation lifestyle under the protection of the country's emperor, Maximilian. Still committed to the ideals of the Old South, he established the largest Confederate colony in Mexico. Unfortunately, Price had walked into an even bloodier conflict south of the border, where he had only a rudimentary understanding of the politics at play.

Maximilian was a foreign adventurer whose government was heavily supported by France. He was fighting his own civil war against supporters of the republican revolutionary Benito Juarez. Under heavy pressure from the United States to withdraw support for Maximilian, the French eventually did so in late 1866, and Maximilian's government collapsed within months. Price and his family, who were under Maximilian's protection, found themselves in desperate straits, needing to flee the country.

In 1867, Price returned with his family to the United States and settled in St. Louis, where admirers bought a house for him. Still an unreconstructed Confederate, he died there on September 29, 1867, and received a hero's funeral.

*

General Sterling Price was a great leader and an accomplished political figure. Because he cared for them, his soldiers loved him and were willing to do anything for him. But he seems to have lacked a clear understanding of the strategic demands of modern warfare.

The accusation that he was a politician's general rather than a professional one is not entirely fair, but it has some basis in fact.

While he was a beloved leader, Price could not improvise a winning

Statue of Sterling Price in Keytesville. According to one of Price's biographers, 15,000 people gathered for the dedication of his statue in Keytesville in 1915. Middle-aged when the Civil War began, Price was widely acclaimed throughout the South for "his victories and skillful retreats," according to historian Mary Ellen Rowe. (Photograph by A. E. Schroeder.)

strategy on the battlefield in the way that Doniphan could. As a Civil War general, he left much to be desired. Price, unlike Ulysses S. Grant who was educated at West Point, was a self-taught general, and the battles fought during the Civil War required professional military leadership. Price did not seem to understand the overall strategic goals he was trying to accomplish with his battlefield tactics. Allowing his forces to get sucked into the battle at Pilot Knob was a blunder that cost him the chance to take St. Louis.

In addition, Price clearly misjudged the feelings of Missourians by believing that they would join his fight to bring Missouri back under Confederate control. His raid into Missouri was the last gasp of the Confederacy in the West. It might have been successful if it had been launched earlier, but the Confederacy did not give him the necessary tools when he needed them. His invasion came two years too late.

Price also shared a basic characteristic of many Southern military leaders, whose primary loyalty was to a particular state. Although the South had many of the nation's best generals, it was often difficult for those generals to work together, especially when the interests of their states differed. The Union could and did play a game of divide and conquer against them.

Conversely, when Union general Ulysses S. Grant was given command of a military unit from Illinois and was ordered to lead those men into Missouri, he didn't question the authority of the federal government to make that decision.

Contrast Grant's actions with those of Generals Ben McCulloch and N. B. Pearce. The Arkansas and Texas generals were willing to help Price defeat Nathaniel Lyon at Wilson's Creek, but they were unwilling to make a long-term commitment to combine forces to retake the rest of Missouri. Instead, they retreated to protect their own states.

When assigned to Tennessee, Price repeatedly requested permission to lead a grand invasion to rescue his own state, even as the other Confederate states were taking the brunt of the war. Davis and other Confederate officers considered such carping to be a sign of Price's selfishness.

Still, one cannot rate Price by the defects of the Confederate system. As with all military commanders, he ultimately must be judged by his results. Price fared well in the Mexican War against ill-trained Mexican troops but not so well in the Civil War against professional soldiers.

In part, his personality and background may have been to blame for his lack of success in the Civil War. Price appears to have been overly concerned with personal honor and soldierly valor, traits that others perceived as vanity. To win, he needed to put aside his ego and study the strategic situation objectively. His situation during the Missouri raid called for restraint against his captured foes, not retribution, of which Missourians had already had their fill. Revenge did not accomplish his objectives.

Price seemed not to realize that he was no longer fighting the Mexican War. His invasion of Missouri appears to have shared many aspects of his earlier jaunt into Mexico, including a vast supply train and a methodical advance of volunteer soldiers. His successful tactics of the Mexican War were no longer effective in this new conflict.

By its end, the Civil War was not about the valiant bravery and gallant virtues on which earlier conflicts had supposedly rested, as Grant and other Union commanders grew to realize. Instead, it was about total war, about killing as many of the enemy and their civilian supporters as necessary to win. It was about breaking the back of the southern economy and the will of southerners to fight, a gloomy portent of modern conflicts to come, but the reality nevertheless.

The new circumstances required a more objective, analytical approach rather than a romantic one based on the ideals of the Old South, and it required well-trained professional soldiers on a well-defined mission, not gallant volunteer adventurers learning soldiering on the job against a weaker enemy.

In the words of fellow Missourian William Tecumseh Sherman, speaking years later, war was hell, and Price's adherence to the earlier romantic view made him a fossil from an earlier age. "It's over; don't you get that? Your times is over," the friendly sheriff told the two outlaws in the movie *Butch Cassidy and the Sundance Kid.* And so it was for Price. The antebellum South Price had fought for was gone forever, and so was he—gone, but not forgotten in Missouri.

For further reading

General Sterling Price and the Civil War in the West, by Albert Castel (Baton Rouge: Louisiana State University Press, 1968), focuses on Price's experiences during the Civil War. Castel argues that even though Price played an integral role in the war west of the Mississippi, he was at best a mediocre general.

Sterling Price: Portrait of a Southerner, by Robert E. Shalhope (Columbia: University of Missouri Press, 1971), documents Price's life, his principles, and his political and military exploits as it delves deeply into his years in Missouri politics. It describes Price as a man trying to adhere to outmoded Jeffersonian values derived from an agrarian aristocracy in a nation that was quickly becoming a modern, industrial, and capitalistic state.

"Sterling Price: Soldier-Politician-Missourian," essay by Rick Eiserman in *Missouri Folk Heroes of the 19th Century,* edited by F. Mark

McKiernan and Roger Launius (Independence, Mo.: Herald Publishing House, 1989).

Sterling Price: The Lee of the West, by Ralph R. Rea (Little Rock: Pioneer Press, 1959), provides a lively and interesting narrative of the general's life. It sometimes leaves out important information as it jumps around in time. Rea's work is more of a personal family history—his ancestor fought with Price—than a biography of Price's life.

4

Ulysses S. Grant

Although he was born and raised in Ohio, Missouri was the adopted home of Ulysses S. Grant. He spent many of his happiest years in Missouri in the 1840s and 1850s, stationed at Jefferson Barracks and living on a farm outside St. Louis. Although he moved to Illinois less than a year before the start of the Civil War, he quickly returned to Missouri to command an Illinois regiment during the opening months of the war and received his promotion to general in Missouri.

Grant first made headlines with the capture of Forts Henry and Donelson on the Cumberland and Tennessee rivers. But his career was defined at the battle of Shiloh in southern Tennessee. It was during this campaign that his trademark fighting style and personality first came into focus.

But Grant's early years showed little of that future promise. Born on April 27, 1822, in Point Pleasant, Ohio, he was the first child of Jesse and Hannah Grant. Jesse was a tanner and businessman who had come from a very poor family, so poor that his father apprenticed him to a tanner when he was eleven years old because the family could not afford to keep him.

Jesse and Hannah named their son Hiram Ulysses Grant. When Ulysses was eighteen months old, the family moved to Georgetown, Ohio. As he grew up, local townspeople in Ohio laughed at his lack of business sense. Throughout his life, Grant repeatedly referred to one particularly embarrassing incident in his childhood. When he was eight years old, he wanted his father to buy him a colt from a nearby farm. His father had offered $20 for the colt, but the farmer said that he wanted $25. Jesse Grant told his son to offer $20, then $22.50, and finally $25 if the farmer simply wouldn't budge. Ulysses reported that he went to the farmer and said, "Papa says I may offer you $20 for the colt, but if you won't take that, I am to offer twenty-two and a half, and if you won't take that, I am to give you twenty-five." Needless to say, the farmer sold him the colt for $25. After the story got out, Ulysses was the laughingstock of the town.

It is difficult to assess the impact that this episode had on him, but he did include the tale in his memoirs as a humorous story about his early life. Whether the incident was important to Grant's development or just an amusing story, he grew to love horses and became well known for his ability to break in new colts. Confederate general James Longstreet, a classmate of Grant's at West Point and his long-time friend, and others mentioned his way with horses. It may well be that Grant's fighting style was forged by the talent that brought him early success in breaking colts. The breaking of a horse requires stubborn persistence, or what President Abraham Lincoln called "dogged pertinacity." You hang on, taking whatever punishment the horse delivers, until the horse realizes he can't win and gives up. That was how Grant would win the battle of Shiloh and how his Union forces would prevail during the Civil War.

A thrifty father, Jesse Grant wanted his son to get a good education at government expense. Hoping he would make a good soldier, since he had shown little aptitude for business, Jesse obtained an appointment to West Point for his son in 1839. Upon his arrival at the military academy, the young man became Ulysses Simpson Grant. Apparently, the senator who had appointed him to the academy did not know that Ulysses was Grant's middle name, and he gave Ulysses on the entry form as Grant's first name. Needing to insert a middle name on the form, he chose Grant's mother's maiden name of Simpson, a prominent family in Ohio. Grant kept the name. Although other boys would often turn Ulysses into "Useless," he still preferred it to Hiram, a name he never liked. After becoming Ulysses S. Grant, he proudly bore his country's initials, which brought him notice from other officers. To fellow West Pointers, his nickname was Uncle Sam.

The name would take on greater significance early in the Civil War when he took Fort Donelson. Trapped in the fort were Confederates under the command of General Simon B. Buckner, a former classmate of Grant's at West Point. When Buckner asked Grant for surrender terms, Grant demanded unconditional surrender from his foe. Although the Confederate commander considered the response unsporting, he accepted, and the Union newspapers claimed a new hero. Playing on his initials, they dubbed him "Unconditional Surrender" Grant.

Grant graduated a mediocre twenty-first in his class of thirty-nine at West Point and showed little potential for any subject except horsemanship, but he did get a good education. After his graduation in 1843, he and his fourth-year roommate, Fred Dent, were both assigned to Jefferson Barracks outside St. Louis. The location was ideal for Dent because his family lived on a farm near the city. Enjoying his stay at the post, Grant spent much of his spare time at the Dent family farm, White Haven, where he fell in love with Fred's sister, Julia. Julia shared Ulysses' love of horses, and she became the true love of his life. She liked the outdoors and enjoyed fishing. Although not considered a ravishing beauty, she was described as lively and determined and a good match in pertinacity for her future husband.

In 1844, returning from his leave in Ohio, Ulysses stopped at White Haven on his way back to join the Fourth Infantry unit in Louisiana to ask for Julia's hand in marriage. They married on his return from the Mexican War in 1848 and had four children, three boys and one girl.

Grant served with distinction in the Mexican War under General Zachary Taylor, another future U.S. president and the father-in-law of Jefferson Davis, the future president of the Confederacy. Although Grant would also serve under General Winfield Scott, the other main Mexican War commander, it was from Taylor that he learned the most about being a general and the importance of results over ceremony. Unlike Scott, who reveled in spit and polish, Taylor believed in informality and simple dress, even while on the battlefield. He would wear blue jeans and a straw hat while on campaign.

After Grant proudly rode through his hometown wearing a sparkling lieutenant's uniform after his graduation from West Point, to the jeers of his neighbors, he took his mentor's example to heart. When Confederate general Robert E. Lee surrendered to Grant at the end of the Civil War, Lee arrived at Appomattox in full-dress uniform. After all, he had been Winfield Scott's protégé in the Mexican War. Grant, however, came dressed in a muddy private's uniform, a Zachary Taylor man to the last.

In his memoirs, Grant said his attire at Appomattox was due to his not realizing that the surrender would come so quickly. "When I had left camp that morning I had not expected so soon the result that was then taking place, and consequently was in rough garb," Grant said. "In my rough traveling suit, the uniform of a private with the straps of a lieutenant general, I must have contrasted very strangely with a man so handsomely dressed, six feet high and of fault-less form. But this was not a matter that I thought of until afterwards."

Grant also followed Taylor's example when dealing with the defeated Confederate army. During the Mexican War, after the battle of Monterey, Taylor had allowed the Mexicans to surrender on good terms, letting them march away with their muskets and artillery, and with their pride intact. Grant would offer similar terms to Lee's men at the end of the Civil War.

Even though he wanted a frontline battle post, Grant served as quartermaster to Winfield Scott's army in its drive to take Mexico City. During this campaign, he served with other officers who would become prominent during the Civil War, including Robert E. Lee, P. G. T. Beauregard, and George B. McClellan. Although he preferred action to managing the equipment, ammunition, and food for the troops, the quartermaster job gave him valuable experience in army stewardship that would serve him well as commander in the Civil War.

Not letting his quartermaster duties keep him away from action on the battlefield, Grant led a successful charge against the enemy at Resaca de la Palma. Similarly, at Monterey, he borrowed a horse and rode to the front, where he joined an attack against a fort that was protecting the city. He found himself in urban combat, darting from house to house in downtown Monterey. The regiment to which he had become attached was running out of ammunition, so he rode

Grant returned to St. Louis after his resignation from the army in 1854 and tried to make a living farming and with various jobs in the city. His father-in-law, Frederick Dent, referred to him as "that trifling, no-good, damned son-in-law of mine," according to Charles van Ravenswaay in *St. Louis: An Informal History of the City and Its People, 1764–1865*. (Missouri State Archives.)

Cheerful through good times and bad, Julia Dent Grant was devoted to her husband and shared with him a love for horses. (State Historical Society of Missouri, Columbia.)

past the Mexican defenders to obtain more ammo, hanging on to the side of his horse with one boot in the stirrup and the other at the back of the saddle, using the opposite flank of the horse for cover.

Later, in the Mexico City suburb of San Cosme, he led an artillery detachment past an unguarded flank of the enemy's line. He placed a light howitzer in a church belfry and rained down shot on the Mexican defenders, helping to break their line and win the battle.

Unfortunately, after his battlefield success in the Mexican War, Grant began to flounder. During the 1850s, he was transferred to the West Coast. Far from his wife and children, he became lonely and depressed and reportedly began to drink heavily. In 1854, according to rumors, he was ordered to resign from the military by his commanding officer or face a charge of drunkenness on duty. Whether or not the rumors were true, having received the honorary rank of brevet captain for valor in the Mexican War, he resigned on April 11, 1854, the same day he was promoted to full captain.

Grant returned to St. Louis and attempted farming on land given to Julia by her father, tried to sell real estate, and then cut and delivered wood to customers in the city. He lived with Julia in a cabin he built himself, naming it "Hardscrabble." This down-and-out period in his life later became known as his hardscrabble years, transformed to legend by later Republican Party campaigns. It was a difficult time for him economically, but although he was poor, this time in his life appears to have been relatively happy. He was with his family, and they were more important to him than money.

The signs of economic hardship in the hardscrabble years are plentiful. There was a local anecdote, perhaps fictional, which later would receive comment in a St. Louis newspaper, that Grant never paid off his bar tab at a local tavern he frequented while engaged in his wood deliveries. There is also evidence that in 1857 he had to pawn his watch to buy Christmas gifts for his family. Historian Bruce Catton points out the irony that an ex-quartermaster and soldier, who would later manage an army as well as any man in American history, could never manage his own affairs, even when those mundane affairs were all he had to worry about.

Grant's father offered him a tannery job in Galena, Illinois, but his heart had never been in that line of work. He had applied, but did not get, the position of St. Louis County Engineer, because of his father-in-law's proslavery views and perhaps because he himself had owned a slave during this time of relative poverty. He bought William Jones in 1858 and freed him in 1859 before applying for the position with the county. St. Louis was already strongly divided on the question of slavery, and the county commissioners were pro-Union.

The Grants moved to Galena in 1860. Bruce Catton suggests that the move was an unconditional surrender to his father's business world. At the very least, his acceptance of the job may have been indicative of the fact that the Grants were in desperate economic straits.

The Civil War broke out a year later. In 1861, with the help of his father and an Illinois legislator, Grant wrangled a command. Nobody knew it yet, but this short, rumpled man who slouched when he walked, sometimes drank to excess, and perpetually chewed a half-smoked cigar would soon shake off his past failures and become perhaps the most successful of all the Union generals. His success on the battlefield would take him to the White House.

Grant was appointed colonel in command of the Twenty-first Illinois Volunteers in June 1861, and his unit was sent to Mexico, Missouri, to guard the Northern Missouri Railroad. On July 11, a small detachment of Confederate troops under Colonel Thomas Harris laid siege to the Monroe Seminary, which was occupied by Union soldiers, in Monroe City. In his first Civil War action, Grant attacked and routed the Confederates from the seminary. "It occurred to me at once that Harris was as much afraid of me as I was of him," Grant said. "That was a view of the question I had never taken before but was one I never forgot."

While in Mexico, according to his memoirs, he learned he had been recommended for promotion to brigadier general via a St. Louis newspaper. Grant was then transferred to Ironton in Iron County, where he prepared to attack Confederate troops based at Greenville, but before he could do so, he was ordered back to St. Louis.

In August, the newly arrived commander of the Western District, General John C. Frémont, ordered Grant to Jefferson City to construct a system of defenses around the capital. Grant quickly realized he was out of his depth and made his displeasure known. He had forgotten most of the engineering lessons from West Point and had no military engineers available. Grant wrote Frémont that he did not want to gain "Pillow notoriety" for incompetence, referring to Confederate general Gideon Pillow, who was infamous for inept placement of fortifications during the Mexican War.

Jefferson City was filled with refugees from nearby counties who were fleeing Rebel bushwhackers whose principal targets were the German farmers along the Missouri River. According to historian Dino Brugioni, German newspapers complained that they were killing not only people with German accents but anyone with a "German face."

The city had five cannons and one hundred rifles but only ten rounds of ammunition per man. Perhaps remembering that the Mexicans had spent too much time on building fortifications and not enough time on training, Grant wrote Frémont that he would not fortify Jefferson City but would focus on instruction instead. His new Jefferson City recruits had been allowed to enlist for various terms and conditions of service and were, he said, "a totally unmilitary lot, lacking in training, without arms and equipment, and bumbling in drill."

After a week in the state capital, he was transferred to Cape Girardeau to take command of the District of Southeast Missouri. Then Grant's Illinois troops were assigned to Cairo, Illinois, a key strategic town at the extreme southern tip of the state where the Mississippi and Ohio rivers meet. When the Confederates entered the neutral state of Kentucky and occupied Columbus, Grant quickly took the city of Paducah, Kentucky, an important step in maintaining control over the Ohio and Mississippi rivers. On November 5, 1861, Grant took 3,000 men down the Mississippi River by boat to attack a Rebel camp at Belmont in Mississippi County, Missouri. His men routed the Confederates but were driven out in a counterattack by superior enemy forces who had also crossed the river from Columbus, Kentucky. There were 642 Confederates and 480 Union men killed during this battle, but both sides claimed victory.

These early engagements were all warmup to Grant's becoming a war hero. His first recognition came after he captured Forts Henry and Donelson on the Tennessee and Cumberland rivers in western Tennessee. Forts Henry and Donelson were strategic, but vulnerable, earthworks along the Confederate western defense line. In tandem

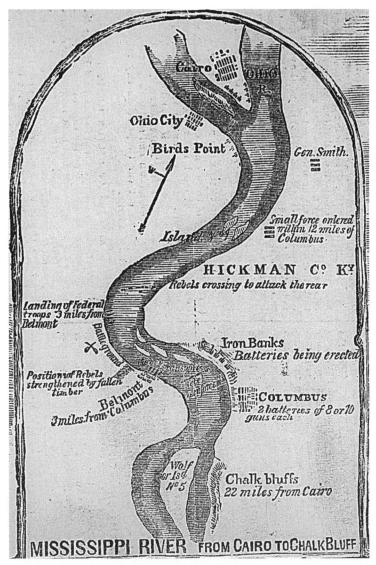

Grant brought troops downriver from Cairo, Illinois, landed near Belmont, and marched toward the Confederate camp on November 5, 1861. A local legend held that as he forced his horse down the gangplank a "hunter from the hills drew a bead upon him" but did not fire, later explaining, "Well, I wasn't right certain it was Grant on that horse." Grant considered the battle won when the Confederates scattered, but reinforcements from Kentucky arrived before he withdrew and caused considerable damage to Union forces. (State Historical Society of Missouri, Columbia.)

with a squadron of ironclad gunboats led by Navy flag officer Andrew H. Foote, Grant transported his army south from Paducah, Kentucky, on the Tennessee River to a campsite north of Fort Henry on February 4, 1862.

Two days later, they attacked, with Grant's forces advancing southward to surround the fort and the gunboats firing on the fort from the opposite direction. The gunboats did their job well, pounding the garrison into submission. After sending the majority of his men, about 2,500, east to Fort Donelson, the Confederate commander surrendered.

After securing Fort Henry, on February 11 Grant's 15,000 troops headed for Fort Donelson and arrived two days later to set up a perimeter around the fort and the town of Dover on the Cumberland River. The next day, Foote's Union gunboats arrived from the north and began an artillery duel with the Confederate batteries covering the river. This time, the Southerners damaged the gunboats so badly they had to retreat.

Grant, however, had been receiving reinforcements and had almost completely encircled the Confederate forces. He now had about 27,000 men facing about 14,500 Confederates. On February 15, the Confederates attacked Grant's right in an attempt to break through, but the attack stalled and Grant counterattacked, closing off the escape route. That night, about 2,000 Confederates escaped, some upriver to Nashville and others with famed Confederate cavalryman Nathan Bedford Forrest.

The next morning, Brigadier General Simon B. Buckner, left in command of the remaining 12,000 troops, asked Grant for surrender terms. "No terms except an unconditional and immediate surrender can be accepted," Grant answered.

"Unconditional Surrender" Grant would now polish his fame at the battle of Shiloh. On the night of April 5, 1862, overconfident and thinking that the Confederates were on the run, Grant chose a campsite for his 40,000 Union soldiers at Pittsburg Landing on the Tennessee River near Shiloh Church, where he was ordered to wait for Don Carlos Buell's Army of the Ohio. He was not expecting an attack by the Confederates, and he planned to move with Buell toward Corinth, Mississippi. His Army of the Tennessee was full of fresh recruits, so he ordered his men to drill rather than to fortify their positions. They drilled, swam in a local creek, and went to bed, thinking the enemy was twenty-two miles away.

Grant's troops awoke at first light to the sound of gunfire as thousands of Confederate troops under General Albert Sidney Johnston charged into their camp, taking them completely by surprise. Some Union soldiers fought back, but many were captured or killed. Most retreated as fast as they could, eventually stopping several miles away at the Tennessee River.

The Union army had suffered some devastating blows in the East, and it appeared that the Union was on the verge of another huge, discouraging defeat in Tennessee. Would Grant join the line of Union losers, those generals who proved themselves unworthy to face the dashing Confederate brass?

Although the odds were stacked against him, Grant decided to stand and fight. At Shiloh, he was now facing the 44,000-strong Confederate Army of the Mississippi, which had taken him by surprise, and the Confederates were driving the Union forces toward the Tennessee River, where they would be trapped and possibly forced to surrender.

The Confederate army pushed Grant's troops back until noon, taking one Union position after another until the Federals established a tenuous line along a sunken road that formed a natural trench. The Rebels charged the position eleven times but were turned back again and again. Because the bullets buzzed around them like bees, the Confederates named the position the "Hornets' Nest."

In *The Blue and the Gray,* Henry Steele Commager quotes an Illinois private Leander Stillwell, who saw Grant in action at Shiloh in the Hornets' Nest and was impressed by the general's courage. Grant was riding past his men on horseback with his staff officers examining the lines, and, as Stillwell recounted, "He went by us at a gallop, riding between us and the battery, at the head of his staff. The battery was then hotly engaged; shot and shell were whizzing overhead, and cutting off the limbs of trees, but Grant rode through the storm with perfect indifference, seemingly paying no more attention to the missiles than if they had been paper wads."

Then Confederate general Daniel Ruggles brought sixty-two cannons into play against the Hornets' Nest. The Rebel infantry swept forward, capturing most of General Benjamin Prentiss's division, which had held up the Confederates for six hours. Although the Union lost a good fighting unit, Prentiss's stand gave Grant time to form a new defensive line near Pittsburg Landing.

As the Confederates swarmed around the Hornets' Nest, continuing to press the attack, the fighting became disorganized, with regiments on both sides disintegrating. Adding to the confusion, the Orleans Guard Battalion joined the battle in their dress blue uniforms, and their fellow Confederates mistook them for Union soldiers. The situation on the Confederate side became even more muddled after General Johnston was killed and General P. G. T. Beauregard assumed command.

With fifty-three guns of his own now placed on the heights around Pittsburg Landing, Grant's position had stabilized. Late in the afternoon, the Confederates attacked again but were easily turned away. The fighting sputtered out around nightfall, and Union gunboats blasted the Confederate positions. During the night, General Buell's army crossed the river to join Grant's, making his army 55,000 strong. When the Confederates attacked again in the morning, the strengthened Union forces pushed them back and went on the offensive. Beauregard counterattacked, stopping the Union advance but not breaking the Union line. Low on ammunition and food, and hobbled by 15,000 casualties, Beauregard withdrew to Corinth, Mississippi. Despite its early setbacks, Grant's army had won a strategic victory by holding on through apparent defeat. Kentucky was now safe from invasion by Confederate forces, and western Tennessee was in his hands. And he would never fall prey to overconfidence again.

A month later, Grant's troops captured the vital railroad town of Corinth and held it against attacks by Generals Earl Van Dorn and Sterling Price. Meanwhile, Union naval forces destroyed the Confederate fleet and captured Memphis. Grant's army moved down the Mississippi to besiege Vicksburg. Known as the "keystone of the West," Vicksburg was important because of its strategic position on the Mississippi River.

On January 30, 1863, Grant took over as commander of operations for the Vicksburg campaign. He first tried to bypass Vicksburg's batteries by digging a canal and by opening various other water routes in the region, including the Yazoo River. After Union acting rear admiral David D. Porter ran his fleet southward past the Vicksburg batteries on April 16, Grant successfully crossed the Mississippi River below Vicksburg with his troops on April 30, and his army won the Battle of Port Gibson the following day. Grant's forces, working in tandem with General William T. Sherman's, slowly tightened the noose on Vicksburg in a siege that lasted six weeks.

Surrounded, the Confederate forces holding Vicksburg surrendered on July 4, making Independence Day celebrations in Washington especially festive. After the fall of Vicksburg, the Union held the Mississippi River, cutting the Confederacy in two. The South now faced a large strategic disadvantage, and General Grant's legend grew.

The possibility of failure did not frighten Grant. He had beaten failure before and knew that if he persevered long enough he would prevail in the end. He was simply unwilling to admit defeat. Lincoln called Grant's stubbornness "dogged pertinacity," and historian Bruce Catton, citing his West Point classmates, labeled it *determination*. Whatever label is applied to him, Grant was a fighter, often taking more punches from his opponent than he gave but refusing to quit until he grabbed victory or the other guy gave up. It was his fighting spirit that appealed to the public.

Although successful on the battlefield and a war hero, Grant was not beyond reproach. He made mistakes, but he usually learned from his errors and rarely repeated them. Perhaps his most famous lapse in judgment was his issuance of General Order Number 11 in December 1862 that forcibly removed Jews from the Department of the Tennessee.

Grant wanted to stop cotton profiteering. Cotton was piling up at southern ports under Union control. Because the Union needed cotton for tents and uniforms, Lincoln permitted limited trade in it but only under special license from the government. Cotton prices were high due to the Union blockade, causing shortages in the North. Northern speculators wanted to purchase the cotton cheap and sell it for a big profit.

These speculators included Grant's father. Jesse Grant visited the general at the front, bringing along his merchant friends, the Mack brothers, who happened to be Jewish, in the hope that he could assure their profit. Furious with his father over the ploy, Grant issued his Order Number 11, expelling all Jews from his jurisdiction in Kentucky, Mississippi, and Tennessee. Enraged Jewish soldiers tried to quit the army in protest, and Jewish leaders protested to the president. Lincoln quickly rescinded the order.

Grant's Order Number 11 is inexplicable because he does not appear to have been particularly anti-Semitic. As president, he appointed Jews to government posts and met with them often. In a misdirected attempt to punish conniving speculators, Grant made Jews the scapegoats. Angry at his father and father's friends, Grant lost his customary calm and rationality, which resulted in an unconstitutional order that tarnished his record, but he appeared to learn his lesson from the episode.

It was not the first time that Grant had displayed his outrage at dishonest speculators. In 1861, at Cairo, Illinois, he threatened to shoot Leonard Swett, a prominent Illinois lawyer and politician, who had nominated Lincoln at the 1860 Republican convention. Using his presidential connections, Swett had pressured Grant to give favors to some contractor friends. But Grant refused to give in to his tactics and told Swett that if he didn't leave his jurisdiction within twenty-four hours, he would put him in prison. When Swett complained to Lincoln about this treatment, the president smiled and advised his friend to stay out of Cairo because from what he had seen, Grant was a man of his word. During his presidency, men like Swett would become the bane of his existence. Too many of Grant's associates, friends, and family members would attempt to influence him for their own gain.

Grant's ability to bounce back from a mistake or lapse in judgment may have stemmed from his ability to choose trusted advisers such as his assistant adjutant general, John A. Rawlins. His advisers, however, could not always keep him out of trouble. In June 1863, while Rawlins was away on business, Grant was interviewed by a *Chicago Tribune* reporter aboard the Union steamer *Diligent*. According to the reporter, the general went on a drinking binge at the bar and had to be escorted back to his stateroom. At one point, the reporter threw away the general's whiskey bottles, but Grant obtained another bottle and got even drunker. When Rawlins returned, he was furious with Grant for his lack of self-restraint.

Although rumors circulated about Grant's drinking, President Lincoln does not appear to have been worried that it would affect his performance. When Secretary of War Edwin Stanton told Lincoln that witnesses had observed General Grant drinking alcohol in his tent, Lincoln replied, "Is that so? Can you tell me what brand of whiskey he's drinking? I want to send a case of it to my other generals."

In March 1864, a couple of months after Grant defeated the Confederates at Chattanooga, Lincoln appointed him general-in-chief of the Union armies. Grant instructed General William T. Sherman to drive across the Deep South while he led the Army of the Potomac against General Robert E. Lee in the Wilderness campaign in Virginia.

As the beginning of a campaign of attrition against Lee's Confederate army, the three-day battle of the Wilderness from May 5 to May 7, 1864, shows Grant's pertinacity in action. Grant did not defeat Lee in terms of casualties—17,660 killed, wounded, and missing for the Union against 7,750 for the Confederates—but Grant could obtain replacement troops while Lee could not.

While past Union commanders retreated after a tough engagement with Lee, Grant immediately resumed his offensive, positioning his forces to attack Lee on May 8 at the battle of Spotsylvania Courthouse, which lasted two weeks, and then on May 31 at the battle of Cold Harbor, which lasted until June 12. Once again, Grant lost twice as many men as Lee in both engagements, an estimated 31,000 total casualties to 14,500 for Lee, but he was wearing down the Confederate forces.

These battles immediately led to the siege of Petersburg, Virginia, which began on June 9 and lasted until March 1865. When Petersburg fell, the nearby Confederate capital of Richmond had to be abandoned soon after, and Lee was forced to surrender at Appomattox Court House on April 9, 1865. Grant had relentlessly used his armies to take the war to the enemy, slowly and deliberately driving them toward defeat.

The stubborn unwillingness to admit defeat that Grant showed in reviving his stalled career and leading the Union army to victory was also evident during his two terms as president of the United States.

Nominated by the Republicans, he was elected to the presidency in 1869. One great example of Grant's dogged determination during

The Lost Cause. Almost four years after the battle of Belmont, on April 10, 1865, General Robert E. Lee surrendered his armies to Grant at Appomattox, Virginia. (State Historical Society of Missouri, Columbia.)

his first term in office was his fight to annex Santo Domingo even after he had lost the political support he needed to make it happen. Historian William McFeely called Grant's fight for the small island nation a "relentless pursuit." While this tactic might work wonders on the battlefield, relentless pursuit is not always the best approach in a political fight. Politicians sometimes need to cut their losses, compromise, and move on. Grant, however, was still fighting for the annexation of Santo Domingo even while writing his memoirs. Battling against death to finish them, he brought up the subject one last time, long after the subject had ceased to be an issue.

In 1869, the black-ruled nation of Santo Domingo on the island of Hispaniola beckoned to Grant. The country, now known as the Dominican Republic, had endured constant political and economic strife, and its wealthy leaders, with little consideration for the needs of their poorer countrymen, thought they could profit by selling their country to the United States. Learning that the U.S. Navy wanted to secure Samana Bay as a base, Grant thought adding the territory would be a good way for the United States to expand into the Caribbean, and he felt it would be an ideal location for ex-slaves from the South to get a fresh start.

Instead of sending his secretary of state to Santo Domingo, which would have been the proper protocol, Grant dispatched his friend and adviser, Colonel Orville E. Babcock, to make a deal. The unofficial way Grant handled the matter led to its eventual demise in Congress and added to the emerging cloud of corruption beginning to taint the Grant administration.

Grant's stubborn fight for the Santo Domingo idea did little to enhance his authority as president. His stubbornness also found expression in his unyielding loyalty to trusted friends and subordinates and his unwillingness to see fault in them when they were under attack. He often stuck by them even when they had acted less than honorably. As president, his blind allegiance to friends who used him for personal gain would stain his administration with accusations of corruption.

Grant had been blessed with a true friend in John Rawlins; Rawlins could tell the general and president things nobody else could. Before the Civil War, Rawlins had been a lawyer in Galena, Illinois, and he and Grant had been neighbors. When Grant did as Rawlins suggested, he usually stayed out of trouble. When he counted on others in the same way, however, the results were less than satisfactory.

Rawlins was Grant's chief aide throughout the war and into his first term as president, when Rawlins also served as secretary of war. In many ways, Grant's friend also functioned as chief of staff at the White House. Unfortunately, Rawlins died of tuberculosis in 1869. Grant chose Orville Babcock, another former officer on his military staff, as an aide. But Babcock was no Rawlins, and he would bring great shame to Grant.

The period after the Civil War, as the nation pushed to modernize, was a time of great public esteem for businessmen with the ability to make vast amounts of money quickly. The administration's first corruption scandal involved two New York financiers, Jay Gould and Jim Fisk. Gould and Fisk wined and dined Grant and managed to bribe his brother-in-law, A. R. Corbin. Corbin's job was to convince Grant not to sell government gold so they could influence its price and reap big profits.

Grant's suspicions were aroused after he received a letter from Corbin suggesting that he not sell government gold. When he learned that his wife, Julia, had received a similar message from her sister, Corbin's wife, he instructed her to write her sister and say, "Tell your husband that my husband is very much annoyed by your speculations. You must close on them as fast as you can."

In what became known as Black Friday, September 24, 1869, Grant ordered his treasury secretary to sell $4 million dollars in gold. The market fell twenty-seven points, resulting in heavy losses to all those involved. Years later, Grant's aide, Babcock, also would be implicated in the Black Friday speculations.

Another serious scandal that occurred during Grant's presidency involved the Credit Mobilier corporation. The affair began before Grant took office, but it came to light near the end of his first term. Credit Mobilier was a railroad construction corporation organized by Union Pacific Railroad Company executives and subsidized by the government. The corporation built the railroad and then set the prices for its use, allowing its stock owners to earn huge dividends, as much as 340 percent of the value of the stock on which the shares were based. Several congressmen and government officials took advantage of the opportunity, including one lawmaker who took 160 shares for himself and gave more stock to his fellow legislators.

Corruption would also rear its head in the administration's Native American policy. At the beginning of his presidency, Grant expressed concern about Native Americans, saying that he hoped to "civilize" them and to make them American citizens. He placed a friend, General Ely S. Parker, who was a Seneca Indian, in charge of the Indian Affairs department.

Under Grant's Peace Policy, Native Americans were to be held on reservations to keep them separated from whites as a protective measure for both Indians and whites, but opportunities for underhanded deals would infect the system. Central to making the process work was the Indian agent, who was supposed to be a governor, administrator, teacher, supplier, and ombudsman all rolled into one. Unfortunately, Indian agents were paid only $1,500 a year, and they were often tempted by opportunities to profit from their positions. Graft was rampant; it was well known that often the supplier who paid the biggest bribe got the contract.

General Parker wound up resigning after two years on the job for allowing such corruption, even though Congress exonerated him personally. Grant would still adhere to the Peace Policy, but the loss of Parker put the Indian issue on the back burner. In addition, public support for fair treatment of Native Americans would dwindle with the defeat of General George Armstrong Custer's Seventh Cavalry by Sioux warriors in the Battle of the Little Bighorn in 1876.

The Belknap affair is one infamous example of the corrupt Indian dealings of some members of the Grant administration. At his friend William T. Sherman's suggestion, Grant named William W. Belknap secretary of war after the death of Rawlins in 1869. A general who had served under Sherman, Belknap had fought at Shiloh.

At the time of his appointment, Belknap was married to his second wife, Carrie, who died of tuberculosis about a year after he took office. Before she died, Carrie had arranged for a friend to get the lucrative Fort Sill trading post contract in Oklahoma. The person holding the contract, however, did not want to give up the job, so the three negotiated a deal in which the contractor would keep the post but would pay Carrie's friend $12,000 a year for the privilege. Carrie was to receive half the money in quarterly payments, and she planned to use the money to pay expenses for her expected child.

When Carrie died a month after the birth of her son, her friend began making the payments to her sister Amanda, who cared for her nephew until the boy died a year later. Amanda continued to receive the payments and later married Belknap after a tour of Europe.

When the news that the Belknaps had received about $20,000 through the unsavory transactions came out during congressional investigations of the Grant administration in 1876, General Belknap confessed to Grant and resigned under threat of impeachment.

The investigations brought the corruption even closer to Grant when newspapers revealed that his brother Orvil, his brother-in-law John C. Dent, and the brother of his aide Orville Babcock also held full or partial ownership in Indian trading posts. Before the corruption investigations ended, Grant's minister to Great Britain, Robert

C. Shenck, had resigned for allegedly taking kickbacks. Secretary of the Interior Columbus Delano and Surveyor General Silas Reed were forced to resign when investigations showed that Delano's son and Grant's brother Orvil had received partnerships as kickbacks in return for awarding surveying contracts that surveyors would not otherwise have received. Likewise U.S. Navy secretary George M. Robeson resigned after allegations that he had received bribes from a grain company. Robeson had made about $320,000 from the deal and had bought himself a new vacation home.

Still, Grant displayed strong loyalty to all of these men until they were eventually proved guilty. For instance, he refused to believe the worst about Babcock, even after his aide had become involved in perhaps the worst corruption scandal of the Grant administration, the "Whiskey Ring."

In 1856, five years before news of the Whiskey Ring scandal broke, Senator Carl Schurz had exposed, in public hearings, some of Babcock's shady dealings. Babcock owned land on Samana Bay in Santo Domingo that would have allowed him to profit greatly if the land had become U.S. territory. Babcock had also developed a relationship with the dictator of Santo Domingo, Buenaventura Baez, that would have kept Baez in power long enough to complete the annexation of his country. To protect Baez's position, Babcock had dispatched U.S. Navy ships to the island to squelch a rebellion, and he did nothing to stop a rival of the dictator from being thrown in prison.

In 1874, newly named Treasury Secretary Benjamin Bristow learned that Treasury employees in St. Louis were taking bribes and cheating the government out of tax revenue from the sale of liquor. The corrupt employees ignored the mismeasurement of bottled whiskey and supplied more tax stamps than the government was actually paid for. Not realizing how close the corruption would come to the Oval Office, Grant told Bristow to investigate the affair.

Bristow and David Dyer, the prosecuting attorney in St. Louis, launched their investigation, and the first person implicated was General John McDonald, collector of internal revenue for the seven-state collection district based in St. Louis. McDonald was a good friend of Grant and of Grant's in-laws. The investigation also turned up evidence against Babcock, but Grant suspected that Bristow and

Dyer were trying to get to him through his friends, and he refused to believe Babcock was involved.

Babcock asked for a military tribunal, and Grant appointed one that would be relatively lenient to him. But Dyer also arranged for Babcock to face a civil trial. To exonerate his friend, Grant hired a private investigator, Charles Bell, to break into Dyer's St. Louis office and arranged to have Bell appointed as a special pension agent in the Department of the Interior to strengthen his position as an official investigator. When Bell eventually found that Babcock could not be cleared and told Grant, the president fired him and continued to support Babcock.

Amid fresh rumors that Grant's brother Orvil and his brother-in-law Lewis Dent, along with Dent's eldest son, also might have been netting money from the whiskey scheme, the scandal swirled around Grant, but he would not budge. He gave a court deposition in support of Babcock, and his friend was acquitted in 1876, appearing to escape blame once again.

But when Secretary of State Hamilton Fish showed Grant concrete evidence that Babcock had speculated in the earlier Black Friday affair, Grant finally asked for his aide's resignation. Babcock's fall came about not because of his involvement in the whiskey scandal but because he had lied to Grant. Meanwhile, McDonald went to jail and wrote a tell-all exposé that was published in the *St. Louis Post-Dispatch*. McDonald charged that Babcock and the Grants should also be in jail because of the whiskey scheme.

Although the scandals were a great embarrassment to the administration, and to the entire country, the Grant administration could claim at least one major accomplishment. In 1871, the government resolved the nation's disputes with Great Britain by successfully concluding a treaty that averted a possible war, which neither country wanted. Hamilton Fish was instrumental in getting the agreement, which settled fishing rights off the coast of New England, fixed the boundary in the northwest between British Columbia and the United States, and got Great Britain to recognize the U.S. citizenship of former British émigrés. It also settled damage claims brought during the Civil War against the British companies that built five warships used by the Confederates to attack the Union blockade of southern ports and other Union shipping.

This triumph, however, hardly outweighed the staggering corruption scandals, and it could never make up for the administration's failure to ease racial tensions in the South during Reconstruction.

In essence, the rampant corruption in the Grant administration had tarnished his presidency so badly that he did not have the political capital to send a large number of troops to enforce the laws upholding black political participation in the South and to control racial violence. The Reconstruction state governments were corrupt, and forced black participation in the political systems of the South only made southern whites more determined to keep the blacks down.

Grant knew the country was tired of war, and his cabinet did not want a race war. In 1875, he sent troops under Philip Sheridan to Louisiana to stop the violence, but he was facing a possible insurrection all across the South. It was, perhaps, the one time in his life that Grant lost his nerve, forging a disastrous compromise that had the effect of allowing southern whites to oppress their black neighbors. While he cannot be blamed for the inaction of later presidents, if Grant had stood firm, the race issue might not have festered for so long afterward.

Near the end of his term as president, Ulysses and Julia considered returning to their White Haven farm in Missouri, but the Whiskey Ring scandals that implicated their St. Louis friends and the high costs of keeping a stable of horses led them to change their minds. Grant's friends wanted to nominate him for a third term as president, but he declined. In 1880 the Republican Party considered him for nomination but nominated James A. Garfield instead. Garfield won the election only to be assassinated in September 1881.

After retiring from the presidency, Grant toured the world with his wife for two years, and then became a partner in his son's financial firm, which eventually went bankrupt after being swindled by his son's partner, Ferdinand Ward. Grant lost his fortune. He had gone from rags to riches and had dropped back to rags again.

Soon after losing his money, Grant learned that he had cancer of the throat. His pertinacity kicked in with a resolve to finish his

In 1886, a marker was placed in Ironton, Missouri, by surviving veterans of the Twenty-first Regiment of Illinois Volunteer Infantry to commemorate the spot where their colonel "Received his commission as General [in] 1861 and parting from his regt. Entered on his career of victory. LET US HAVE PEACE." (Photograph by John C. Fisher.)

memoirs while the tumor slowly choked off his air supply. He held off death just long enough to finish the memoirs, hoping that the proceeds from the sale of his book would support his family after his death. He died a couple of days after completing the last page in 1885.

During the last few years of his life, writing his memoirs and magazine articles about his campaigns, Grant struck up a friendship with Samuel Clemens, whose pen name was Mark Twain. Clemens helped Grant negotiate a more lucrative contract for his memoirs and helped him with some editing of the work.

"I can't spare this man—he fights," Abraham Lincoln said after the battle at Shiloh, and Grant fought until the very end. Ironically, it was his cigar smoking, not his drinking, that brought the cancer that finally did him in. Grant had been a successful general, a war hero, and a mediocre president. But to the end, he was a fighter.

For more reading

Grant: A Biography, by William S. McFeely (New York: W.W. Norton, 1981), paints a picture of Ulysses S. Grant as an ordinary man who had difficulty in finding his true calling.

Lincoln and His Generals, by Thomas Harry Williams (New York: Alfred A. Knopf, 1952), is an excellent book about how Lincoln developed a modern command structure and how he came to choose Grant to command the Union army.

Memoirs and Selected Letters, by Ulysses S. Grant (New York: The Library of America, 1990), is a must-read resource, not only for Grant's accounts of his Civil War battles and presidential memories, but also for his firsthand insight into topics such as the Mexican War.

President Grant Reconsidered, by Frank J. Scaturro (Lanham, Md.: University Press of America, 1998), provides a good counterpoint to those historians who tend to paint Grant as a buffoon. Scaturro argues that Grant was not as bad a president as some other historians have led us to believe.

Ulysses S. Grant: Politician, by William B. Hesseltine (New York: Frederick Ungar Publishing, 1957), is an extensive biography that presents a good portrait of Grant's early and later life.

U.S. Grant and the American Military Tradition, by Bruce Catton (Boston: Little, Brown, 1954), is a quick and enjoyable read about Grant. It gives a good overview of Grant's life and helps in understanding Grant's character.

5

John J. Pershing

John J. Pershing was born and raised in Laclede, Missouri. Before he became a military man, Pershing worked as a rural schoolteacher but aspired to be a lawyer. He attended West Point because it was an inexpensive way to gain a good education. He was a longtime admirer of General Ulysses S. Grant and achieved a military career that rivaled that of the Civil War hero and president.

Although he had dreamed of a law career, after West Point the army way took hold of him. This onetime schoolteacher would become America's top soldier, and his nation would make him the only soldier other than George Washington to attain the rank of General of the Armies.

A strict disciplinarian, Pershing was known for his adherence to regimented, spit-and-polish military rules and for keeping a cool head under fire. These traits enabled him to defeat and then to win over Philippine natives, chase bandits in Mexico, and deal with personal tragedy. And they would serve him well as he created and trained an army that would finally defeat the Germans in World War I and lay the foundation for the United States military power that would help win the Second World War.

Pershing has been described as practical, driven, stubborn, and unsentimental. Never beloved by his troops, but always respected, he was an authoritarian who liked to bark orders but did not like to

A young John J. Pershing poses with his family. His father and mother, John F. Pershing and Ann Thompson Pershing, and his sister Margaret are seated. Standing are John J. Pershing, May, Elizabeth, Ward, and James. Missouri has preserved Pershing's boyhood home in Laclede as a state historic site and established Pershing State Park nearby. (State Historical Society of Missouri, Columbia.)

delegate too many duties to subordinates. According to Richard O'Connor, one of Pershing's biographers, a newsman once said of Pershing, "I didn't much like the old General of the Armies. I had known Chicago gangsters who were friendlier." In Pershing's defense, he didn't like reporters much either.

He was known as a harsh taskmaster, and much of his reputation for hardness appears to have been gained in France during World War I, a few years after the tragic death of his wife and daughters in a house fire at the Presidio in San Francisco. There were really two Pershings: the dashing young officer, tough and disciplined, yet compassionate toward his men, and the older, hardened general who emerged after this tragedy.

Young Pershing was much like the swashbuckling Horatio Hornblower, the British naval officer created by C. S. Forrester in a series of books, but Pershing wore a U.S. Army uniform and cavalry spurs. He used his ingenuity, bravery, and cool head to get out of scrapes, just like the characters in the dime novels he enjoyed reading as a child. But after the death of his family, he became more machinelike, a professional soldier to the extreme, an efficiency-driven commander pushing his men forward with seemingly very little feeling for them.

Pershing was born September 13, 1860, just two months before the election of Abraham Lincoln. His mother, Ann Thompson Pershing, was descended from Virginians. His father, John F. Pershing, was a railroad foreman, farmer, and shopkeeper of Alsatian-German ancestry—his name had been anglicized from the original spelling of "Pfoerschin"—and a staunch supporter of the Union, as were many Americans of German heritage.

One of John J. Pershing's earliest memories involved the day a squadron of William Quantrill's Confederate bushwhackers led by a Captain Clifton Holtzclaw rode into Laclede and shot up his parents' house. His father survived the attack because his mother stopped the elder Pershing from foolhardily charging out the front door with his shotgun blazing.

Pershing's family was relatively well off after the Civil War until his father lost most of their money in the panic of 1873. He had placed the family fortune almost exclusively in local farmland, and when land prices dropped, the Pershings lost all but one farm. John had to take care of the farm while his father found work as a traveling salesman.

John finished his schooling and took a job as a janitor for the two "separate but equal" elementary schools in Laclede—one for black children, the other for white. He then became an elementary school teacher, first at Laclede's black school and then in Prairie Grove. He quickly gained a reputation for imposing strict discipline. When the father of one of his students brandished a revolver and challenged

Pershing over his punishment of the farmer's son, Pershing told him to put his gun away and fight like a man. Then he gave the father such a beating that he had to take him to a doctor.

Pershing attended the State Normal School at Kirksville for two years and received a bachelor's degree in scientific didactics. In July 1881, he began studying law, but he heard that a preliminary examination for entrance into West Point was being given in the nearby town of Trenton and decided to take it. He did so well on the exam that he was nominated over eighteen competitors. Still, to make sure he was ready, he decided to attend a preparatory school for six months before entering the military academy the next summer as a plebe.

More mature than many of his classmates, he was elected first captain of the cadets. As first captain, he marched the cadets to the railroad tracks to salute General Grant's funeral procession as it passed on its way to New York, a final act of respect to an officer whose style of fighting Pershing admired. Another of his influences was Academy Superintendent Wesley Merritt, a hero at Gettysburg, who instilled in Pershing his belief in the value of military discipline and drill. Although Pershing had trouble with French and with speaking in front of his English class, he was class president for all four years.

After his graduation in 1886, thirtieth in a class of seventy-seven, Pershing received orders to Fort Bayard in New Mexico, where he chased Geronimo and other Apache raiders around the Southwest with the Sixth Cavalry. Once again the disciplinarian, he punched an insubordinate trooper who was shirking his duty. He became an avid poker player, showed prowess at working with Missouri mules, and spent time reading and learning Indian languages.

He had to learn a few lessons the hard way. Once when he charged too far ahead of his men, an Indian warrior, hiding behind a rock, knocked him off his horse. Luckily, rather than taking his life, the Indian only stole his gun.

After his transfer to Fort Stanton, Pershing spent time exploring the Sierra Blanca area of New Mexico with two other young officers and met Sheriff Pat Garrett, who six years earlier had shot Billy the Kid. In May 1889, Pershing was ordered to resolve a difficult situation that arose on a nearby ranch. Three horse thieves had stolen from the Zuni Indians and had killed three Zunis before getting away. The Zunis pursued the thieves and surrounded them in a ranch house, threatening to kill them. Pershing convinced the Zunis not to attack. Kicking in the door of the ranch house and charging in with pistols blazing, he forced the thieves to surrender.

The next year, Pershing was sent to the Pine Ridge Indian Agency in South Dakota to help quell the Ghost Dance uprising of the Sioux nation. The Sioux under Chief Sitting Bull were taken by a religious fervor, believing that a messianic leader would come to disperse the white man, revive the buffalo, and bring back to the Native Americans their free life on the Plains. After Indian police in mid-December shot Sitting Bull, a native civil war began that culminated at the Battle of Wounded Knee on December 29, in which the U.S. Cavalry slaughtered 150 Sioux men, women, and children. Pershing was nearby, helping to cordon off an area to keep in the Sioux rebels, and skirmished with an escaping band under Chief Kicking Bear near Little Grass Creek. On the way back through the Dakota Territory, his good planning helped save his men when a severe blizzard hit. They were properly equipped to survive the weather because Pershing had insisted on requisitioning warm overcoats, oversocks, and overshoes before leaving Pine Ridge.

In 1891, Pershing was sent to drill student cadets as a military science instructor at the University of Nebraska. He was well liked by his students, and he made it popular to be a soldier. His student drill team, later named the Pershing Rifles in his honor, won the army's silver cup in competition, second only to the cadets of West Point. In the 1920s, the group joined with similar organizations to become the National Society of Pershing Rifles, which is headquartered in Lincoln, Nebraska.

But Pershing did not want to appear to the faculty as just a soldier; proud of his teaching skills, he also taught courses in math, and he earned a law degree. While in Lincoln, he made civilian friends who would later help his career, including a future governor of Cuba and future vice president, Charles G. Dawes. Dawes would also later serve as Pershing's chief purchasing agent for the army in France.

In 1895, he was promoted to first lieutenant and assigned to command a unit of the Tenth Negro cavalry at Fort Assinboine in the Montana Territory. This unit was charged with rounding up Cree

Indians and escorting them to Canada. His service with the Tenth gave Pershing an appreciation for the abilities of black American soldiers, whom he later led into battle.

A year later, General Nelson A. Miles, who had commanded him in New Mexico, made Pershing his aide-de-camp in Washington, D.C., and then had him posted as an instructor at West Point. A politically connected general, Nelson was married to the daughter of Ohio senator John Sherman, the brother of General William T. Sherman. Interested in advancement, Pershing learned much from Miles about the political aspects of his occupation. While observing a military tournament from a friend's box at New York's Madison Square Garden, Pershing made perhaps the luckiest contact of his life when he met future president Theodore Roosevelt, who would become his chief benefactor. Pershing was Roosevelt's kind of guy—rough, rugged, and schooled in the ways of the vanishing West—and they became fast friends.

Curiously, Pershing was not as popular with the cadets at West Point as he had been at Nebraska because of his harsh discipline, which included his invention of the "jumping jack" as a new way to torture cadets. As a prank, one cadet placed a bucket of mop water over a barracks door as a booby trap for him. When another cadet whispered a warning not to open the door, Pershing sent a janitor to investigate, and the janitor sprang the bucket on himself instead. The angry janitor pressed charges, and the entire company received a sentence of thirty days confinement to barracks, which made Pershing even less popular with his cadets.

It was around this time that Pershing's cadets began to call him "Nigger Jack" because he repeatedly praised his Tenth Cavalry unit and compared their exemplary soldiering qualities with those of his underachieving West Point cadets. The name eventually evolved into "Black Jack," a nickname that both Pershing and the newspapers liked. Aptly describing his kind of soldier, Black Jack combined a hard-hitting combat weapon, his Tenth Calvary service with the Buffalo soldiers, and his fondness for card playing all in one nickname.

While Pershing was at West Point, the war with Spain broke out. The U.S. government wanted naval bases in the Caribbean and Pacific, and Spain's bases were seen as relatively easy to take. When the American battleship *Maine* blew up in the Havana, Cuba, harbor—possibly through equipment failure or by detonating an old mine—the U.S. had its excuse for war. Pershing appealed to the secretary of war for a combat command and was sent back to the Tenth Cavalry as its quartermaster. His post was similar to Grant's position during the Mexican War. While quartermaster, he witnessed the appalling lack of planning for the Cuban expeditionary force, in which too few men were sent to Cuba on too few transports, wearing cold-weather uniforms in a tropical theater, eating rancid tinned beef and wormy or moldy bread, and fighting with inferior weapons. In addition, the army's top brass—seen by many to be old, fat, and lazy—had provided little in the way of facilities to care for the sick and wounded. Nevertheless, Pershing would hear no complaints and dressed down younger officers for bad-mouthing their superiors.

The newspapers exposed the military's lack of preparedness for the operation and its incompetent organization; the experience brought a Senate committee investigation led by Senator Grenville Dodge of Iowa after the war. The investigation led to much finger-pointing and blame, which diminished the career of Pershing's mentor, General Miles.

Future president Theodore Roosevelt, leader of the volunteer Rough Rider regiment, experienced the supply and leadership problems personally. He also had the opportunity to interact personally with his favorite officer. One day, Pershing happened upon Roosevelt and his wagon, which was stuck in the mud, and pulled it out with the help of his mule team.

Later, during the battle of San Juan Hill, Pershing's Tenth Cavalry charged up the hill along with the First Cavalry and Roosevelt's Rough Riders. The fortifications on the San Juan Heights, of which San Juan Hill was a part, were the key to the Spanish position in the city of Santiago. Pershing's Tenth Cavalry lost half its officers and one-fifth of its enlisted men in the charge on July 1, and the campaign gave Pershing new respect for the fighting capabilities of his African American troops. Within a few weeks, Spain surrendered, and Pershing received a promotion to captain. Pershing's courage attracted the attention of Roosevelt and prompted Pershing's commanding officer to say he was the coolest man under fire he had ever seen. Pershing received the Silver Star for his valiant actions on San Juan Hill.

The Cuba supply debacle had made it clear to Pershing, Roosevelt, and the government that the nation's army must be better organized if the United States was to become a world military power. President William McKinley named a new secretary of war, Elihu Root, who began to reorganize the army. Root saw what was needed, but his recommendations would not be fully implemented until Pershing applied the ideas in the deployment of the American Expeditionary Force years later in World War I.

The United States also had taken the Philippines from Spain, but ruling it was another matter. Secretary Root needed lawyers to administer the new island territories and generals to subdue native rebels who had decided to test the mettle of the new regime. Having studied law in Nebraska, Pershing was well qualified on both counts and was recalled to Washington to join the Bureau of Insular Affairs.

After Pershing endured eight months of desk duty, Root sent him to the Philippines, where he served first in an administrative capacity. Soon he made his mark as military commander of Iligan on the north coast of the island of Mindanao, where he showed a talent for pacifying Moros from various tribes. He participated in a couple of punitive expeditions and encouraged tribesmen not to join in rebellion against the new administration.

Pershing made a concerted effort to study the Moros' language and customs, and, by doing so, he won their admiration and respect. He became so knowledgeable about their culture that, even though he was a junior officer, he was given command of Camp Vicars, the main headquarters in that part of the Philippines. The Moros even named him a "datu," a minor noble.

Just as he had been able to win the loyalty of the black soldiers, he got along with the Moros, playing chess with them and learning about their culture: this helped him achieve his goals, but sometimes he used their culture against them. Once when he was having trouble signing a treaty with a local chieftain, he brought in pigs' blood as a threat. He had learned that the Islamic Moros feared pigs' blood, believing contact with it would mean being barred from heaven.

His biggest expedition during his Philippine service came when he decided he had no choice but to use force against the Moros living around Lake Lanao because his attempts at diplomacy had failed. In a campaign that was compared in the press to Confederate general Jeb Stuart's cavalry ride around the Union army, Pershing fought battle after battle, subdued several Moro chiefs, and was hailed as a military genius. He lost only twenty-five men in the campaign, mostly to disease. By the time he was recalled to Washington in 1903, he had become a national hero.

Big changes were being made in the war department that would soon transform Pershing's career. The mistakes made in supplying and leading the forces in Cuba and the Philippines had shown that the military desperately needed to modernize. It was to be reorganized under a general staff model like the one the Germans had employed. As a prod to improvement, President Teddy Roosevelt also began to shake up the officer promotion system, which was based on seniority. This system, he said, "promoted mediocrity over excellence."

While in Washington, Pershing attended the Army War College and kept busy with social engagements. One such event was a ball at which he met his future wife, Helen Frances Warren, the daughter of influential Wyoming senator Francis E. Warren. Before long, Pershing asked Frances for her hand, but she made him wait a year before agreeing to marriage, as was the custom. The final spur came when he was assigned to be the new military attaché in Tokyo. Theirs was the 1905 celebrity wedding of the year. President Roosevelt attended, and headlines heralded the event. The headline in one Philadelphia newspaper read "Army's Only Datoo Wins at Love Too."

His marriage launched a relatively idyllic ten-year interval for Pershing, a decade of wedded bliss in the Far East. The couple had four children: Helen was born in 1906, Anne in 1908, Francis Warren in 1909, and Mary Margaret in 1912. Pershing doted on his children, spending time with them whenever possible.

Pershing's new job was as a military observer during the Russo-Japanese War in Manchuria, where the Japanese were defeating the armies of Czarist Russia. The outside observers were not allowed to see too much, because the Japanese did not want to share military information. But Pershing did see trench warfare in action, which helped him later on the western front during World War I. He began to realize that new advancements in warfare would mean longer battles and would require much larger numbers of soldiers than in the past.

Pershing returned to Tokyo and then was recalled to the United States. During his young family's journey home, President Roosevelt made a decision that shook up the army bureaucracy. He promoted Pershing and fellow officer Leonard Wood from captain to brigadier general, jumping them several grades in rank past hundreds of other senior officers. The move, which President Roosevelt even mentioned in his State of the Union address, caused great controversy and may have added to Pershing's need to make himself more remote from his troops to prove that the jump was merited.

In December 1906, Pershing was assigned again to a command in the Philippines. While he was en route to Manila, his rivals in the military circulated a scandalous story to the press to discredit him. Allegedly, Pershing had lived with a Filipino woman on his first tour in the Philippines, had fathered two children with her, and had offered her $50 a month in hush money to keep her quiet. Although Pershing's rival Leonard Wood affirmed the story in his diary, the captains who had served with Pershing in the Philippines said it was not true. Pershing never commented one way or the other.

In the Philippines, Pershing served as commander of Fort McKinley. In 1908, he was sent on a tour of Europe to inspect the armies of the European powers. After a trip home to visit Hot Springs, Arkansas, for treatment of an illness called sprue, he returned to the Philippines in 1909, where he was appointed military governor of Moro province. Pershing set up several irrigation projects and worked to improve the local living conditions and economy, but after repeated incidents of violence, he decided he had to disarm the Moro tribesmen.

In 1911, upon hearing news of his intentions, the natives on Jolo Island rebelled, and a band of dissident Moros fled to a nearby volcano crater to hold out. After a long siege, they surrendered, but another group tried the same tactic a year later. Pershing responded with another siege. After months of negotiation, he decided to move in. He placed troops between the Moros and their village of noncombatants, surrounded the fort, and slowly closed in on it from all sides. Finally, after enduring attacks from Moros fiercely charging the siege lines, Pershing ordered his forces to storm the fort. All the Moros inside—men, women, and children—were slaughtered.

With the area quiet for now—the Moros would rebel again four years later, armed with repeating rifles—Pershing left for his next assignment, as commander of the Presidio, a military base in San Francisco. A civilian administrator succeeded him in the Phillipines, and the Pershings sailed for home in December 1913. Before he left, according to newspaper reports, the Moros elevated him to the rank of sultan, an honor given to very few white men and the only such honor ever awarded to a U.S. officer.

When Pershing received command of the Presidio, it was a tense time in the Southwest because of unrest in Mexico. In April 1914, U.S. Army troops occupied the city of Vera Cruz, Mexico, after the corrupt government of General Victoriano Huerta had detained an American naval officer. Huerta had seized the government from the beloved Francisco Madero the year before. Pershing's Sixth and Sixteenth infantries were sent by train to El Paso to patrol the Mexican border and to prepare for possible invasion. Pershing reluctantly joined his men, leaving behind his wife, who had been in an automobile accident three days before.

The months in El Paso dragged on, with Pershing monitoring events south of the border. Huerta had been deposed by Venustiano Carranza, who was now facing one rebel group led by Emiliano Zapata in the south and two others in the north under Generals Alvaro Obregon and Pancho Villa. Then in August 1914, to further complicate matters, World War I started after the assassination in Sarajevo of the Austrian archduke Franz Ferdinand.

It was in this pressure cooker atmosphere on the Rio Grande that Pershing received the news that tore his life apart. On August 27, 1915, about a week before his wife and family were to join him in El Paso, Pershing received a telegram telling him that his wife and all three daughters had died in a fire in the commander's quarters at the Presidio. A spark, either from the fireplace or a nightlight, had ignited a new coat of varnish that had been applied to the floor in the house at Pershing's command. His six-year-old son, Francis Warren, was his family's only survivor.

It was perhaps the one time in his life that he had not been in the

A fire at the Presidio in California resulted in the deaths of Pershing's wife and his daughters Helen, Ann, and Margaret. Pershing was commanding the Eighth Infantry Brigade on the Mexican border at the time of the tragedy. (*San Francisco Chronicle*, August 28, 1915, courtesy State Historical Society of Missouri.)

Pershing with his son, Warren, who survived the August 1915 fire that took the lives of his mother and three sisters. (State Historical Society of Missouri, Columbia.)

right place at the right time. Although the experience helped him empathize with others who had lost family members, after this tragedy Pershing appeared even more remote and hardened. He retreated into his professional duties. First, he would deal with the Mexican bandit Pancho Villa, and then he would tackle the Central powers to help win the Great War in Europe.

For some time, Villa, who had tried to effect reforms in his country, had been a U.S. favorite in the struggle for leadership in Mexico. But he had been showing increasing pro-German tendencies. Looking for a way to keep the United States occupied so that it would not enter the European war, the Germans began to finance Villa's efforts in an attempt to influence him to lead his movement in an anti-American direction.

According to historian Barbara Tuchman, the Germans had been meddling in Mexican affairs for years before and during World War I in an effort to keep the United States from joining the war in Europe on the side of the Allies. They had orchestrated a failed attempt to oust Carranza and to bring Huerta back to power, and they even tried to coax Japan into joining the Central powers and using Mexico as an avenue of attack on the United States.

In 1915, concluding that promoting stability south of the border and foiling German schemes were more important to U.S. diplomatic aims than keeping Villa as a friend, President Woodrow Wilson recognized Carranza's government in Mexico, making Villa an outlaw. The U.S. also supported an attack on Villa's forces in September by providing rail transport for Carranzistas across the American Southwest. The attack killed 85 percent of the Mexican bandit's troops.

In retaliation, on January 10, 1916, one of Villa's lieutenants pulled nineteen Americans from a train near Santa Isabel in Chihuahua and executed them. Pershing had to send troops to El Paso to stop a riot at the train station when the bodies arrived. Villa claimed his men acted without authorization, but then he showed his true colors by leading a raid on Columbus, New Mexico, at 4:15 a.m. on March 9, 1916. Villistas killed several soldiers and rode up and down the streets on horseback firing guns into houses and throwing torches into businesses. The U.S. Army troops stationed there fought back and won the exchange despite being taken by surprise. Villa left 215 of his men dead on the streets of Columbus. On the American side, fifteen soldiers and civilians were killed and thirteen were wounded.

President Wilson ordered the army, with Pershing in command, to apprehend Villa but "with scrupulous regard for the sovereignty of Mexico." The order put Pershing in the unenviable position of violating Mexican sovereignty by crossing the country's border in force to find a bandit protected by the local populace and a government that hated gringos meddling in its internal affairs. Neither Villa nor Carranza wanted the American troops in their country, and the forces of both sometimes conspired against Pershing's efforts. His primary objective was not to start a war with Mexico, a difficult directive for a general commanding an invasion force. Nabbing Villa was his secondary objective.

Pershing's columns fought the Villistas several times. In one widely reported incident, George S. Patton, who would later become famous as a tank commander in World War II, killed three of Villa's top men with his Colt .45 Peacemaker in true Wild West gunfight fashion after being ambushed at a farmhouse. Patton tied the dead Villistas to the hood of his jeep and triumphantly drove back to camp as if he had been on a hunting trip and had taken three prize bucks. In another engagement, two overzealous units of the Tenth Cavalry on a scouting party decided to attack a force of Carranzistas at Carrizal. The Carranzistas outnumbered the Americans four to one and badly mauled them, killing one captain, gravely wounding another, and taking twenty-three men prisoner.

In the end, the governments found a diplomatic solution. Pershing never caught Villa, but the mission was declared a success nevertheless, and the U.S. forces evacuated in late January and early February of 1917. Within a few weeks, Pershing was promoted to major general and placed in command of the Southern Department of the army after the death of the former commander. Although it was hardly a success, the Villa operation served as a dress rehearsal for Pershing's next challenge as commander of the American Expeditionary Force to Europe in World War I.

The sinking of the *Lusitania* and the *Sussex,* the resumption of unrestrained submarine warfare by the Germans, economic ties to the Allies, and Allied propaganda all played a role in bringing America into the Great War a few months later. But the final straw that led President Woodrow Wilson to declare war on Germany was an intercepted message from Germany's foreign minister, Arthur Zimmerman, to Mexico. The Zimmerman telegram, published in newspapers on March 1, 1917, proposed that Mexico and Japan join an alliance to attack the United States and offered the Mexican government money and the return of its former territory in the American Southwest. According to historian Barbara Tuchman in *The Zimmerman Telegram,* a subsequent note, which was not released to the public, made clear that the offer to Mexico was immediate, not hypothetical or contingent on the U.S. entering the war in Europe.

The United States declared war on Germany in April 1917. Pershing was called to Washington a month later and given command of the American forces in France. President Wilson felt he could follow orders and keep his opinions to himself. The other most likely choice, General Leonard Wood, was a staunch Republican with political aspirations, and he had criticized the president in public. Later, after Wood pulled strings to get to France, Pershing requested that Wood be sent home.

Pershing quickly sailed for England. After arriving, he enjoyed great acclaim, with parties in his honor and dignitaries clamoring to

General Pershing with a group of dignitaries in France. In a light uniform, leaning on his sword, he is talking with Marshall Joseph Joffre, the president of France. (State Historical Society of Missouri, Columbia.)

meet him. He then moved on to France to launch the new American Expeditionary Force. Wilson's orders were to build an American army to fight under an American command.

Pershing enthusiastically organized his army. If the United States was to be treated as an equal among the Allied forces, its military force needed to be as skilled as the European armies. Otherwise, American soldiers would simply be integrated into the British and French armies—the course the Allies wanted the United States to follow. Pershing saw right away, however, that trying to blend American soldiers in with existing foreign units was not in America's best interest. Over the long haul, the American public would not want to play second fiddle to the Europeans, and President Wilson had made it clear that he wanted an equal seat at the peace table so that he could make the world better through a spirit of cooperation and goodwill.

The task facing Pershing called for a manager. As biographer Richard Goldhurst wrote in *Pipe, Clay and Drill*, Pershing's realization that war is above all a managerial enterprise made him the founder of the modern American military tradition. Pershing's foresight helped the United States mobilize when World War II came two decades later. Without the logistics experience gained by Pershing's staff in France, and without the selective service experiment in the First World War, it is highly likely that the United States would have been even less ready than it was when it entered World War II. The landings on D-day, as costly as they were, might have been worse without the knowledge of French infrastructure gained in World War I.

It has been said that the American war effort in World War I amounted to fifteen months of fighting in the rear and two months of fighting at the front. America's raw recruits were slowly shipped overseas and equipped and trained by Pershing in France before they were sent to the front. To the British and the French, this training period seemed endless, and they questioned its usefulness. Why were the Americans wasting so much time creating their own military training program? Why waste so much time trying to make every private into a Pershing? Why not just train them alongside British and French soldiers and then integrate them into British and French armies?

Pershing had to fight Allied efforts at integration constantly, and the Allied prime ministers continually complained to the president and war department about slow training that never seemed to produce American soldiers at the front lines. But Pershing knew the British and French were dispirited from years of defeat. Their generals constantly quarreled, and they no longer had the stomach to take the war to the Germans and push them out of France to claim victory on their own. By 1918 the British were tired of fighting, and the French were demoralized and on the brink of collapse. Many of the French army units were already mutinying. A pessimistic mood prevailed on the streets of Paris. The war had been going on for four years, and millions of French soldiers had been killed. With the Russians now leaving the fight, the full weight of German and Austrian forces would come to bear against the western front. France's sole hope lay in a new supply of American troops who could turn the tide and drive the Germans back, or at least negotiate a truce. If the war was to end soon, the United States would need to take the initiative, which meant the U.S. needed its own army. Furthermore, the U.S. would need its own army after the war if it wanted to have a part in peace negotiations and greater status as a world power. So Pershing stuck to his guns.

Pershing also struggled with Wilson's chief of staff, General Peyton March, over who was in charge. Among other things, they fought about whether American doughboys should wear the Sam Browne belt, a leather belt—named for a British general who used it in India—with a shoulder strap to help carry the weight of a heavy pistol or sword. It was worn by officers, but March saw little practical value in its use because the army also issued a cloth pistol belt, which was much easier to use. But Pershing loved the Sam Browne belt for its martial look. He won that fight and the battle with March over his request for eight regiments of cavalry, even though they proved to be of little use against machine guns.

As it turned out, Pershing could not completely control the use of American troops by the Allies. The Germans launched a series of offensives in the spring of 1918. They were hoping to end the war before a significant number of American soldiers could begin fighting alongside the Allies, and they almost succeeded. German troops attacked the British across the Somme and Lys rivers, smashing the British Fifth Army beyond repair. In the Aisne sector, the Germans launched an offensive against the French, taking 65,000 French prisoners and routing the rest. The Germans reached as far as the Marne River, as they had in 1914. Seeing that the British and French armies were in danger of collapse, Pershing let some of his units attach themselves to French and British commands. The two divisions he sent to Marshall Henri Pétain at Château-Thierry kept the Germans from crossing the Marne.

On May 28, 1918, the Americans won their first offensive action of the war, against the Amiens salient, a part of the battle line projecting forward, at the village of Cantigny. Under heavy bombardment, the Twenty-eighth infantry took and held the village. With the French running from a German advance, American troops plugged a hole in the line at the Paris to Metz highway and pushed the Germans back, driving them all the way out of Belleau Wood.

The Germans kept mounting offensives over the next month or so, but the Allied counterattacks were taking their toll. The Germans tried again to cross the Marne, but the French attacked, with the Americans spearheading the advance. An American assault on the Soissons plateau caught the Germans by surprise, and they eventually had to retreat from the Marne.

During the summer of 1918, the Americans broke the back of the German offensives, and the Germans retreated along the entire front. Then it was time to take the battle to the enemy. Pershing announced the formation of his 550,000-man First Army on August 10 and took over the St. Mihiel sector. Two days later, his men would go over the top.

The French tried to get Pershing to change his plans for the American offensive at St. Mihiel, with Marshal Ferdinand Foch appealing to him to join an Allied offensive farther north. Although he had to agree to join the larger northern offensive in two weeks, Pershing persisted in following his own plan. He wanted the American forces to gain a complete victory in the attack on the St. Mihiel salient, which had jutted into the French lines since 1914.

American troops descended from both sides of the salient and trapped the Germans inside. The attack was a success, with the advancing Americans taking 16,000 German prisoners and 450 guns and forcing the Germans back to the Hindenburg Line. Even Pershing's cavalry did well. Although unseated by the machine gun fire, they advanced on foot and captured ten Germans. The advance might have continued all the way to Metz if Pershing's army had not had to stop to join Foch's offensive in the North.

Lieutenant Colonel George C. Marshall, a Pershing protégé, planned the logistics and led the mass switching of American for French armies along the line to prepare for Foch's offensive in the Meuse-Argonne. He became known as "the wizard" because the movement came off without a hitch. Pershing assumed command of the Meuse-Argonne on September 22 and launched an attack with 600,000 men four days later. It would be one of the longest, toughest American battles ever fought and in terrain much like Grant encountered in Virginia in the Wilderness campaign during the Civil War.

For three days the Americans were successful, taking German positions and the village of Montfaucon before getting bogged down. In rough fighting with heavy casualties, the Americans kept up the pressure. Meanwhile, even though the British were not moving as quickly, they were also advancing in Flanders.

During this fight, the Seventy-seventh Division, the "Lost Battalion," commanded by Major Charles Whittlesey, gained fame by advancing too far into the Argonne Forest and getting cut off. They refused to surrender and eventually American troops rescued them.

Before long, the Americans had driven a wedge into the German lines, and the First Division, the "Big Red One," took the crest of Montrefague. Douglas MacArthur, commanding the Eighty-fourth brigade of the Forty-second "Rainbow" Division, discovered a hole in the barbed wire and exploited it to outflank the German position. Although he often complained about the lack of spit-and-polish discipline within the Rainbow division, Pershing lavished praise on MacArthur for this effort.

As Pershing kept pressing his men forward, the Hindenburg Line began to crumble, and the German navy mutinied at Kiel. The Allies broke the German lines again on November 1 and raced the Germans all the way to Sedan. Unfortunately, a mixup in orders occurred on the way, and two American divisions headed for the same place and fired on each other. Douglas MacArthur, now a brigadier general, wearing informal clothing, was mistaken for a German officer and captured.

The American and French armies also accidentally crossed into one another's sectors and almost attacked each other until the generals realized what was happening. The Americans backed off, and the French took Sedan first, breaking the German communications in the Lorraine area. On November 10, the German Kaiser fled to Holland, and the next day, at the eleventh hour of the eleventh day in the eleventh month, a negotiated armistice went into effect. Pershing had won the war in the battle of the Argonne, at great cost in American casualties, but the war was over.

Although his American Expeditionary Force would stay in the Rhineland until 1923, Pershing headed home in September 1919. Elevated in rank to General of the Armies, he took a ceremonial tour around the United States before replacing General March as chief of staff. Ironically, his new role would mean supervising the dismantling of the victorious military machine that he had built.

While in Washington, Pershing pursued a vivacious widow, Mrs. Louise Cromwell Brooks, amid rumors that they were unofficially engaged. In January 1922, however, Brooks broke Pershing's heart by announcing her engagement to the forty-two-year-old superintendent of West Point, General Douglas MacArthur, who was twenty years Pershing's junior. Although Pershing denied the story later in the press, Mrs. Brooks said he tried to dissuade her and suggested she marry one of his colonels because he did not like MacArthur. When she refused, he warned her to be ready for the Philippines, the post to which MacArthur was assigned six months after the wedding. Whether there was any connection is a matter of dispute; in any event, she and MacArthur divorced six years later. Meanwhile, Pershing continued to see Micheline Resco, a young Parisian artist with whom he had carried on an affair during World War I. He secretly married her in 1946.

Pershing retired in 1924 at the age of sixty-four and spent the next twenty years traveling between the U.S. and Europe, working on part-time presidential assignments and helping his young protégés move ahead. For instance, when the new chief of staff Douglas MacArthur transferred George Marshall to the Illinois National Guard, Pershing worked to get him a better post.

When his health began to fail in 1941, he moved into Walter Reed Hospital in Washington to spend the final years of his life, keeping up with world events from his hospital room. During World War II, he wrote to President Roosevelt, suggesting he keep General Marshall in Washington and send General Dwight D. Eisenhower to lead Operation Overlord, the invasion of Europe, advice that Roosevelt followed.

Pershing died early in the morning July 15, 1948, at the age of eighty-eight, of arteriosclerosis and a heart attack. He was buried in Arlington National Cemetery with the pomp and circumstance befitting the nation's second General of the Armies.

Although never adored by his men, Pershing became the model of the supremely confident and capable modern military man who earned respect because of his coolness under fire and his ability to get things done. Pershing can be seen as the personification of the U.S. Army's coming of age. His career ran the gamut from kicking in the doors of Wild West horse thieves fleeing the law to managing the intricate logistics and movement of a vast American army on another continent. The role of the U.S. Army changed in similar fashion, from policing a wild frontier to policing a new empire. Pershing blended the best of the old army with equipment and tactics that would meet the needs of a new century of warfare and the demands of America's new role as a world military power.

When Pershing attended West Point, the curriculum had a heavy emphasis in engineering. The army wanted men who could function in a variety of roles, rising to the challenge of any situation they faced. In a United States that was quickly mechanizing, a soldier was just one more cog in the machine. Pershing took this message to heart.

The Spanish-American War showed that the machine was falling apart, and Pershing gained the experience to recondition it for World War I by scrimmaging against Pancho Villa. Yet, even though the army had new weaponry, Pershing still tended to use his armies in the same way as had his fellow cavalryman and hero, General Ulysses S. Grant. Pershing beat the German army by hammering it in the Argonne, persevering until it surrendered. The strategy worked, but it produced heavy casualties.

Pershing knew how to play politics and how to use the press. As his critics have pointed out, he was a politician's general, and his rise in the ranks was directly connected to his ability to garner friends in high places. His allies in the political and military higher echelons constantly and methodically groomed him for ever loftier positions of responsibility. To Pershing's benefit, influential newspapers of the time desperately wanted a hero to write about during the Spanish-American War and the American campaigns in the Philippines and in Mexico. Although often testy with reporters, to some extent Pershing the hero was their creation.

Pershing's bold stand against the Allies—his insistence that America would fight only under its own leadership as a distinct force—makes him the architect of American military supremacy in the twentieth century. Although his crowning achievement came in World War I as the commander of the American Expeditionary Force in France, his most lasting contribution may have been in developing the officers who would later succeed him. Many of America's top generals in World War II, including George Marshall and George Patton, were his protégés and absorbed much of his work ethic, discipline, and competence.

In some ways, Patton and Marshall personify the two most notable aspects of Pershing's character. From the beginning of his career, as a young lieutenant chasing Villistas under Pershing, Patton patterned himself after his boss. He adopted the swashbuckling soldiering style of Pershing's earlier career and made it his own. During World War II, he adapted cavalry tactics to tanks and rode the metal beasts to fame.

Marshall absorbed Pershing's astute attention to detail, a trait that caused Pershing to be habitually tardy. Pershing learned, through his observation of the supply disasters of the Cuban and Mexican expeditions, his participation in the Punitive Expedition against Pancho Villa, and his successful campaign in World War I that the modern general facing twentieth-century conflict would have to be a good manager above all. Marshall became the consummate manager—better than Pershing. In tandem with his political skills, he moved beyond his military career and became a successful cabinet member of the Truman administration.

But Pershing's flaws kept him from transcending his military career. Biographer Richard O'Connor said he had two main deficiencies: he lacked the ability to inspire his men and possessed an overly strong conservatism that tended to lead him to reject unorthodox views held by unconventional men, along with new weapons and tactics. He did not understand Patton's fascination with tanks, he did not want to give up on the cavalry, and he thoroughly misjudged the possibilities of air power and its main proponent, General Billy Mitchell.

Pershing could not make the move into politics because he did not have the requisite political skills. He was never a politician. Several times during his bureaucratic battles behind the lines, he proclaimed that he was only interested in military matters, declaring he was there to fight and that he left the political decisions to the generals in Washington. Politics was too messy and too disorderly. It involved too much compromise and deal cutting.

Therefore, unlike Grant, Pershing was unable to translate his fame as a general into the presidency. He halfheartedly entered the Nebraska primary for the Republican nomination in 1920 and came

General John J. Pershing is considered, according to historian C. David Rice, to be "one of America's premier soldiers and one of Missouri's proudest contributions to the nation." He was a soldier "who could keep his head when all around him were losing theirs." In 1921, Potsdam in Gasconade County changed its name to Pershing to honor him. (Missouri State Archives.)

in a distant third. While the mood of the country had turned against the military, if Pershing had been a particularly charismatic leader, he certainly would have made a better showing. In retrospect, he may have made the best choice in not pursuing higher office. Unlike Grant, at least he ended his career on a high note.

Pershing is the father of the modern military organization and of America's role as the world's preeminent military power. A soldier through and through, he served his country and safeguarded its interests, sacrificing much along the way. This coolheaded icon, the most famous general of his day, subdued the Philippine natives, fought on San Juan Hill with future president Theodore Roosevelt, dealt with unrest and revolution in northern Mexico, and defeated the Germans in World War I. But in many ways his most lasting contribution was in developing the modern army that would successfully defeat the Axis in World War II.

For more reading

Black Jack Pershing, by Richard O'Connor (Garden City, N.Y.: Doubleday, 1961), is an excellent account of Pershing's life that delves especially well into the politics between the Allies and their chief generals in World War I. The book discusses Pershing's role in laying the foundation for America's preeminent military power in the twentieth century and assesses the personality traits that did not allow him to move beyond the military into politics.

My Experiences in the World War, by John J. Pershing (New York: Frederick A. Stokes, 1931). This is Pershing's memoir, which received the Pulitzer Prize for history in 1932.

Pipe Clay and Drill: John J. Pershing: The Classic American Soldier, by Richard Goldhurst (New York: Reader's Digest Press, 1977), is an especially well-written biography of Pershing. This work tends to focus less on World War I and more on other parts of the general's life, providing details and context that other biographies do not give about his place in the military tradition, his mentors, and his recognition of the importance of the general as manager in the modern international conflicts of the twentieth century.

Until the Last Trumpet Sounds: The Life of General of the Armies John J. Pershing, by Gene Smith (New York: John Wiley and Sons, 1998), tells the story of the strict disciplinarian who, after a lengthy military career in the Pacific, lost his family in a tragic fire and later led the American Expeditionary Force to victory in World War I. It also suggests that his greatest legacy may have been in developing the next generation of generals who would fight in World War II.

6

Omar N. Bradley

Although he was not one of General Pershing's protégés, Omar N. Bradley's story parallels that of his World War I forerunner, and he and other World War II commanding generals benefited greatly from Pershing's experience in World War I as they planned and executed the invasion of Europe and other campaigns. Taking on much the same role as Pershing did during the First World War, Bradley led the American forces to victory against Nazi Germany.

The press dubbed Bradley the "G.I. General," because reporters could see he cared deeply about the plight of the common soldier. As a boy, his military heroes had been George Washington, Robert E. Lee, and Ulysses S. Grant. Like these men, Bradley became a hero to many Americans. A 1945 story in the *St. Louis Globe-Democrat* compared him to Grant, Lee, and Stonewall Jackson and said he was "the nearest thing to Abraham Lincoln in uniform the American Army has ever produced."

Omar Nelson Bradley's ancestors emigrated from Great Britain to Kentucky in the mid-1700s and moved to Missouri's Randolph County in the early 1800s, settling near what would become the towns of Clark and Higbee. His grandfather served in the Confederate army, and his father, John Smith Bradley, was a rural schoolteacher known for his ability to discipline wayward farm boys. From his father, Omar Bradley gained a lifelong love of hunting, fishing, and baseball.

Portrait of Omar Bradley from the Moberly High School Yearbook, 1910. (State Historical Society of Missouri, Columbia.)

John Bradley married Sarah Elizabeth "Bessie" Hubbard in 1892, and, nine months later, on February 12, 1893, Omar was born. He was named for two local family friends: "Omar," a newspaper editor, and "Nelson," a doctor. As a small boy, he gained instant older sisters when his aunt died and her daughters, Nettie and Opal, moved in. His younger brother, Raymond, died of scarlet fever as a toddler.

The family moved frequently as his father went from one teaching post to another. They walked everywhere because they did not own a horse and buggy. Omar liked to read, especially books such as *Ivanhoe* and *The Jungle Book*. His father taught him to shoot, buying him first a BB gun and then a .22 rifle. Omar became such a good shot that he hunted and dressed rabbits for sale.

When Omar was twelve, his family bought a small house at a sheriff's auction in the town of Higbee. To help make ends meet, Omar, his mother, and the girls operated a rural phone line. Omar and his father also laid traplines for fur, gathered honey from hollow trees, and dug yellowroot to sell for making medicines.

Bradley in 1915 in his United States Military Academy uniform. (Gift of James T. Brockman, State Historical Society of Missouri, Columbia.)

In January 1908, when Bradley was fifteen, his father died of pneumonia. His family moved to Moberly, Missouri, and his mother became a seamstress and took in boarders. Bradley attended Moberly High School, where he played baseball and ran track. In Moberly, he also joined the Christian Church, delivered newspapers for money, and met his future wife, Mary Quayle.

Bradley was a good student, and, like Pershing, he wanted to study law but could not afford college. He worked for the Wabash Railroad trying to earn enough money to attend the University of Missouri. When his mother remarried on Christmas Day 1910, he no longer had to worry about her security. When a family friend told Bradley about West Point, he was very interested, especially after learning that if accepted he could attend for free. A recent change in the law allowed his congressmen to nominate a second candidate, giving Bradley a chance to get in, but he first had to take the entrance exam right away in St. Louis and score better than another candidate who wanted the appointment. With a free ticket from the

Wabash Railroad, he hopped the train, reviewing his books on the way, and took the exam. On July 27, 1911, he received a telegram that notified him that the appointment was his. He was given five days to report to West Point.

Bradley loved West Point and did not even mind the hazing because it put everybody on the same level. His class of 1915 would become known as the "class the stars fell on" because of the number of generals it produced.

After graduation, he came home, and, by the end of the summer, he and Mary Quayle were engaged, with a wedding date set for June the following year. That fall of 1915, the army sent Bradley to the Fourteenth Infantry regiment, based at Fort George Wright in Spokane, Washington. In his free time, he studied small-unit tactics and military history and served as defense counsel for men who had been AWOL (absent without leave). On May 11, 1916, the army called his regiment to the Mexican border. At the same time, his fiancée caught typhoid fever, and they had to postpone the wedding. With Pancho Villa on the loose, and the Germans pressuring the Mexican government to attack the United States, the army was ready for war across the Rio Grande.

Mary moved to Columbia, Missouri, to attend college, and she and Bradley were married there on December 28, 1916. After a short honeymoon in Kansas City and Los Angeles, they returned to his post at Yuma, Arizona. Four months later, President Woodrow Wilson declared war on Germany, and the army ordered Bradley to Vancouver Barracks, Washington.

Although he desperately wanted an assignment in France, Bradley was soon sent to Butte, Montana, where he policed copper mines, prevented labor unrest, gave speeches to sell bonds for Liberty Loans to the Allies, and fought forest fires. Finally, on September 25, 1918, his unit was ordered to Camp Dodge in Des Moines, Iowa, to train for combat in France, but the armistice with Germany was signed on November 11. The war had come and gone, and Bradley had missed it. Demobilizing quickly into a peacetime force, the army sent Bradley to Camp Grant near Rockford, Illinois, then to a teaching post at a ROTC unit at South Dakota State College, and later to West Point.

At West Point, Bradley met General Douglas MacArthur, who

had served as commandant at the school since 1919. He liked it that MacArthur liberalized the curriculum, stressed physical fitness, and abolished hazing, but he did not approve of the new relaxed discipline and MacArthur's decision to let a standout football player with failing grades remain on campus. More important, army chief of staff John J. "Black Jack" Pershing did not approve of MacArthur and exiled him to the Philippines after the younger general married Pershing's potential bride, Louise Cromwell Brooks. Although the incident did not affect Bradley at the time, it would serve as a precursor to future confrontations with MacArthur.

At West Point, Bradley taught math, coached football, and studied General William T. Sherman's ideas on rapid "movement" warfare; he supplemented his salary with earnings at the poker table. Mary gave birth to their only child, Elizabeth, on December 3, 1923. Bradley then moved to the Infantry School at Fort Benning, Georgia, where he became a disciple of the war of movement advocated by Sherman and Pershing, who used the tactics to break out of the stalemated trench warfare of World War I. He placed second in the advanced course, while his classmates, who had served in the static World War I trenches, had trouble with the concepts.

In August 1925, Bradley received command of an infantry regiment in Hawaii. There he met Major George S. Patton when he joined Patton's trapshooting team. When his infantry command was finished, Bradley spent another year in Hawaii as liaison officer for the Hawaiian National Guard. After returning to the mainland in 1928 to attend the Command and General Staff School at Fort Leavenworth, Kansas, for a year, he decided to return to Fort Benning instead of going back to West Point. It turned out to be the best career decision he ever made.

The assistant commandant, Lieutenant Colonel George C. Marshall, one of Pershing's most trusted subordinates, was shaking up Fort Benning's curriculum. Later, Marshall's era at Fort Benning would be seen as the "nursery school" for the generals of World War II. Bradley became Marshall's protégé, just as Marshall and Patton had been Pershing's protégés. He taught officers, at Marshall's insistence, to simplify orders so that America's citizen soldiers could understand them, to welcome unconventional ideas, to take advantage of an opportunity when they saw it, instead of waiting for orders from above, and to be resourceful in turning around an unexpected setback.

The good times came to an end, however, after the stock market crash of October 1929. Not only did the Great Depression bring budget cuts and reduced pay for the military in 1930, but President Herbert Hoover named Douglas MacArthur as the army's new chief of staff, and MacArthur transferred George Marshall to the Illinois National Guard as payback to the aging Jack Pershing, thus turning the Pershing-MacArthur feud into a Marshall-MacArthur feud. The bad times were further accentuated for Bradley when his mother died of a stroke in May 1931.

In 1933 Bradley attended the Army War College near Washington, D.C., where he honed his planning skills and played war games for a year before becoming a senior instructor in the tactical department at West Point and receiving a promotion to lieutenant colonel. In 1938, as General Chancellor Adolf Hitler absorbed Austria into his Third Reich and invaded Czechoslovakia, the army sent Bradley to join the War Department's general staff as assistant secretary under now Chief of Staff George Marshall.

World events unfolded quickly. Germany signed a landmark non-aggression pact with the Soviet Union, and the two countries invaded Poland. Britain and France declared war on Germany and waited for Hitler's next move. Hitler rapidly invaded Denmark and Norway; attacked the Netherlands, Belgium, and France; and forced Britain to evacuate its trapped army from Dunkirk in May 1940. Italy invaded southern France, the Germans occupied Paris, France surrendered, and Nazi Germany began the Battle of Britain by air and at sea.

In response, the United States began building its armed forces by calling up the National Guard and Reserves, instituting a draft, and training new units. In February 1941, Bradley became commandant at Fort Benning. Skipping over the rank of colonel, he was the first in his class to be promoted to brigadier general. At Fort Benning, Bradley organized the first Officers Candidate School (OCS), a new prototype training program for civilians wanting to become junior officers, and oversaw training of new armor and airborne combat units.

On June 22, 1941, Hitler broke the German-Soviet nonaggression pact by invading Russia. The Soviet Union then joined the

Allies. On December 7, 1941, the Japanese attacked Pearl Harbor and subsequently took over Southeast Asia and much of the Pacific. The next day, the United States and Britain declared war on Japan, and, on December 11, Germany and Italy declared war on the United States. As a matter of strategy, the Allies decided it would be best to defeat the Germans first.

Quickly promoted to the rank of major general—the second in his class to earn two stars—Bradley received command of the Eighty-second Division and was assigned Matthew Ridgway as his assistant division commander. Knowing he needed to get the men in shape, Bradley designed a tough obstacle course for everybody, including himself. His men shared a good laugh at his expense when the forty-nine-year-old general slipped off a rope into a sewage pit. To inspire his men, Bradley brought in Eighty-second Division alumnus Sergeant Alvin C. York, who was famous for single-handedly capturing 132 German prisoners during the battle of the Argonne in World War I. York startled Bradley when he told him he was "too nice" to succeed as a general.

Without warning, Bradley was ordered to hand the Eighty-second over to Ridgway, who would convert it into an airborne division, and assigned to get the Twenty-eighth Infantry, a National Guard division from Pennsylvania, into shape. Bradley's new division was rife with "hometown-ism." Because of friendships or professional connections to the fathers of their soldiers, the division's leadership at various levels often did not impose appropriate discipline on its men. Bradley solved the problem by ordering all division officers and noncommissioned officers to transfer to other units so that an outfit's officers, noncoms, and soldiers would not come from the same town.

Bradley also implemented a rigorous physical fitness program, which included a twenty-five-mile hike in full gear that everyone—including Bradley—had to complete. The men built up to the hike in stages. Bradley took the twenty-five-mile test wearing standard fatigues without rank insignia. Men dropped out right and left, but Bradley arrived at the finish line carrying the packs and rifles of several men who barely made it. Not realizing who he was, a soldier asked him, "Who the hell ordered this march?" "I don't know, but they ought to hang the S.O.B.," Bradley answered. The line was later used in the movie *Patton*.

The media did not know what to make of Bradley. He was not colorful; he cared about his men and was professional. While the press was slow to recognize it, the prototype of the American general had shifted to emphasize teamwork and personnel management skills, and Generals Marshall, Eisenhower, and Bradley set the new standard.

On February 16, 1943, Bradley received orders to join General Eisenhower in Africa, where he began to understand the incredible role intelligence would play in the Allied war effort. Early in World War II, the United States cracked the Japanese diplomatic code, which the Americans referred to as "Purple." It was decoded for the Allies under the code name "Magic." In Europe the Poles had managed to steal a German Enigma machine, which all German military units used to transmit information, and gave the machine to the British. Although the Germans did not believe that it was possible to do so, the British used the machine to decipher the German coded radio traffic. The Allies referred to the German decoded intelligence as "Ultra." With expert interpretation, the intelligence helped the Allies predict where and when the Axis powers might attack. This worked especially well when the intelligence that the Americans took from the Magic decodes backed up information the British gathered from the Ultra decodes.

As Bradley came to learn, Ultra helped create the early Allied hero of the war, British general Bernard L. Montgomery. Monty, as he was called, used the decoded intelligence to defeat Erwin Rommel's Afrika Korps at the battle of El Alamein in Egypt. Beloved by the British, the flamboyant and media-savvy general was considered by American GIs to be a "glory hound," going out of his way to look like a hero. Bradley grew to loathe Montgomery and faulted the British general for his slow execution of battlefield operations. His plans were usually elaborate, but he would spend so much time preparing for an attack that his attack would come too late and too slowly, allowing the enemy to better defend itself. At El Alamein, Montgomery had knocked Rommel down but failed to deliver the final knockout blow, a pattern the general would follow again and again until Germany's final defeat.

Bradley reached North Africa just after Operation Torch, during which American troops had landed at Casablanca, Oran, and Algiers. The Americans pushed the Germans eastward, while Montgomery's forces pushed westward, eventually cornering the enemy in Tunisia. The Germans, however, had routed the untested Americans at the battle of Kasserine Pass, and General Marshall sent Bradley to find out what was wrong at the Tunisian front. After observing operations there, Bradley conferred with Eisenhower, who decided to relieve General Lloyd Fredendall, put Patton in command of Second Corps, and make Bradley Patton's deputy commander.

As Bradley watched Patton whip his soldiers into shape, he found his fellow general's treatment of his men excessively harsh and often lacking in judgment: Bradley saw Patton lose his temper and scream at his men in front of his superiors, Eisenhower and Marshall. In Tunisia, while inspecting the headquarters of General Terry Allen's First Division, the "Big Red One," Patton viewed the men's slit trenches, used for cover from enemy aircraft attacks, with obvious contempt. In full view of all, Patton unzipped his fly and urinated into Allen's trench. "Now try to use it," Patton sneered, implying that real men did not need trenches. For the rest of the war, Bradley often would have to deal with bizarre behavior from both Patton and Montgomery.

Slowly, the Allies cornered the Germans in Tunisia and pushed them toward the sea. The German Tenth Panzer Division attacked the Americans at El Guettar, but, with a day's advance warning from Ultra intelligence, Bradley helped prepare defenses to stop the Germans and avenge the Kasserine defeat.

Constant friction between the British and Americans simmered under the surface of outwardly friendly relations between the Allies. Montgomery broke through the German lines and could have surrounded and trapped the enemy, but he moved too slowly and lost the opportunity. Bradley and Patton also complained about the lack of British air support for American troops and about Eisenhower's favoring the British, whose battle plans for the final conquest of Tunisia only gave the Americans a supporting role.

Bradley took over the final push in Tunisia when Patton headed back to Morocco to prepare the First Armored Corps for the upcoming invasion of Sicily, Operation Husky. The men loved it when he eased some of the more oppressive regulations from Patton's reign of terror, which had only allowed breakfast to be served for fifteen minutes at six o'clock in the morning and forced medical staff to wear helmets.

Through tough fighting for the city of Bizerte, Bradley's men showed they were just as skilled as the British soldiers when they captured 250,000 Germans. To the press, Montgomery claimed credit for the victory in Tunisia, but Bradley also began to get noticed. He was popular with the Arabs, who mistakenly thought that one of their own, a good Muslim named Omar, was leading the American armies. Seasoned in Africa, the U.S. Army would now invade the Italian island of Sicily, where *Washington Daily News* correspondent Ernie Pyle, encouraged by Eisenhower, "discovered" Bradley for a six-part series published in Scripps-Howard Newspapers in the States.

Bradley watched Patton and Montgomery compete over the invasion plans; Montgomery won, due to Eisenhower's pro-British bias, Bradley believed. Bradley thought Montgomery's Operation Husky plan was flawed. Patton's plan had called for the Americans to land on the western end of the island, with the British and Americans converging on Messina, while Montgomery's plan put the Americans in a subordinate role protecting his left flank. In addition, Bradley believed that both sides of the Messina Strait between mainland Italy and Sicily should be taken at the same time to trap the Germans on the island.

The first phase of the invasion plan involved deceiving German intelligence in Operation Mincemeat. On April 30, 1943, a British submarine launched the body of a supposed Royal Marines officer off the Spanish coast. In a briefcase chained to his wrist were documents detailing an Allied invasion of Sardinia, Corsica, and Greece, with a minor attack on Sicily. As intended, spies in Spain found the body with the plans. Ultra intelligence showed that Hitler had taken the bait and had sent reinforcements to these areas detailed in the fake documents but not to Sicily.

World War II's first Allied airborne drop came the evening of June 9, 1943, and it was not very successful. High winds and darkness confused the pilots, and many planes got lost or dropped troops in the wrong place. A second airborne assault turned deadly when U.S. Navy gunners accidentally fired on their own planes.

Bradley's troops hit the beach early the next morning, landing on the central southern coast, while the British landed on the east. Many Sicilians quickly surrendered and even agreed to unload ships in exchange for not being sent to a POW (prisoner of war) camp. The main problem came in unloading heavy tanks and artillery, which sank in the soft beach sand. Luckily, U.S. Navy battleships firing from offshore stopped a Panzer tank counterattack.

The Patton-Montgomery rivalry took its toll on Bradley. Poised to make a breakout that might have allowed him to envelope the enemy, take Messina, and shorten the Sicily campaign by weeks, Bradley's plans were stymied when Montgomery changed the battle plan without informing the other commanders and pushed Bradley's troops westward, taking for himself a road assigned to Bradley's forces. Bradley was infuriated.

Since nobody stopped Montgomery from making his own plans, Patton decided to do the same. Ignoring orders from the British general in charge of the operation and vowing to beat his English rival to Messina, Patton roughly followed his original invasion plan, taking Palermo on the west coast of the island and then heading across the northern coast road to Messina. Patton's plan left Bradley having to march northward through the center of the island through difficult terrain and tough opposition without support.

Heading east along the north coast road, Patton linked up with Bradley. They met fierce resistance, and Bradley came up with the idea of outflanking strong enemy positions through small amphibious landings. They tried the maneuver three times. The first try took the Germans by surprise but came too late to catch a withdrawing Panzer Division. The second turned disastrous when men were needlessly lost because Patton refused to postpone it twenty-four hours, having already invited the press. The third was unnecessary, because the land-based soldiers were advancing quickly, but Patton insisted on holding it for publicity reasons. The amphibious forces ended up landing amid Allied troops. Luckily, nobody was killed by friendly fire, but eleven men drowned in a landing craft accident.

Bradley would soon witness two of Patton's most notorious public blunders that would derail the older general's career and lead to Bradley's future promotion. Already under fire from Eisenhower for infrequent reports and for visiting the front after repeated warnings not to do so, Patton again lost his temper during two visits to field hospitals. Enraged at a young private with battlefield fatigue, Patton called him a coward, slapped him in the face with his glove, and threw him out of the tent, shocking everyone inside. It later turned out the private suffered from chronic diarrhea, malaria, and a 102-degree fever. Patton next assaulted a soldier with shell shock, calling him a "goddamned coward" and a "yellow son of a bitch," then threatened to shoot him on the spot, pulling out a pistol and waving it in the soldier's face. When the soldier began to cry, Patton hit the private so hard that his helmet liner flew off and rolled out of the tent. Such uncontrolled behavior was soon to lead to Patton's professional undoing.

By August 10, the Germans were cornered in Messina. Bradley wanted the Allies to use air and sea power to trap the Axis forces on Sicily, as the French fleet had trapped the British at Yorktown during the American Revolution. Instead, the Allies failed to act, letting 110,000 Germans evacuate to fight again.

Pushing hard to beat Montgomery to Messina, Patton ordered Bradley to get there first even if it cost extra lives. Bradley ignored the order and kept making whatever maneuvers were necessary to safeguard the lives of his men. On August 16, American troops reached the outskirts of Messina, but they were not allowed to enter until Patton could arrive for a parade and surrender ceremony, which meant silently watching the remaining German soldiers escape. At 10 a.m. the next morning, Patton showed up. He asked why everybody was standing around, then led a motorcade into the city and held a surrender ceremony in a park, one hour before a British column marched in. Patton had won his race to Messina but at a terrible cost of life—5,532 killed, 14,410 wounded, and 2,869 missing. His many lapses in judgment, especially those publicized by the press, led Eisenhower and Marshall to pass over Patton and choose Bradley to command the upcoming invasion of France.

The Allies had finally agreed to invade France. General Marshall, whom Eisenhower would then replace as chief of staff in Washington,

Bradley, *ca.* 1944, with General Dwight Eisenhower and General Courtney Hodges. It was in Hodges's sector at Remagen that the Allies first crossed the Rhine. (U.S. Army photograph, courtesy State Historical Society of Missouri, Columbia.)

would lead Operation Overlord. Bradley headed for London, first stopping to say goodbye to Patton. He found his former commander depressed: he had also been passed over for command of the Italian campaign, and his army was being dismantled.

Bradley flew to the United States to gather staff, meet with General Marshall, and confer with President Franklin D. Roosevelt, who told Bradley about the secret atomic bomb being developed. Allowed to visit his family, Bradley learned his daughter was planning her wedding in June, at the same time as the upcoming invasion of France. For security reasons, he could not tell her that he would be unable to attend.

Back in London, Bradley prepared for the invasion. Marshall wanted to lead Overlord, and President Roosevelt wanted Marshall to be the hero of World War II, but the public would view his transfer to Britain as a demotion. Meanwhile, Eisenhower wanted the Overlord job, and he had worked well with the British. After Stalin accused the British and Americans of stalling in setting up a second front, Roosevelt decided he needed Marshall in Washington and named Eisenhower to command Overlord. The decision created a good team: Marshall the manager, Eisenhower the diplomat, and Bradley the tactician.

Eisenhower arrived in London as the supreme commander on January 15, 1944, with D-day in Normandy set for May 1. To the Americans' displeasure, the British chose Montgomery as Eisenhower's ground force deputy; he would command all forces as they hit the beach. As additional armies came ashore, Bradley would lead an American army group, a command equal to Montgomery's.

Patton became a decoy, commanding a fake army in southeast Britain seemingly poised to invade France in the Pas de Calais region. Through Ultra, the Allies knew that Hitler believed they would invade at Pas de Calais, so they planned to invade Normandy instead. Unknown to the Nazis, the British had taken over the German spy network in England and used it to reinforce the hoax that they would invade at Pas de Calais.

Once the invading force was established, Patton would join Bradley in France, but once again Patton's mouth nearly got him sent home instead. First he reportedly suggested to troops in Sicily that they should shoot Germans who tried to surrender. Then he gave a supposedly off-the-record speech to ladies in Knutsford, England, in which he seemed to suggest that the United States and Britain were destined to rule the postwar world, without mentioning any role for the Soviet Union.

Such distractions may seem frivolous now, but they might have led to military disaster. Bradley did not need to face German defenders who continued to fight for fear of surrendering. Failure on D-day would mean another full year of preparation, and it would give Hitler time to deploy secret weapons. Russia might lose faith in her allies and sue for a separate peace with Germany.

According to the invasion plans, upon landing the British would take the left and the Americans the right. Montgomery's forces were to seize Caen, while Bradley's army would move inland, cut the Cotentin Peninsula, and pivot to take Cherbourg. The Canadians would then come ashore to reinforce the British, and Patton would arrive to reinforce Bradley, whose army would then wheel southeastward toward the Loire River.

After several delays, the D-day invasion finally began on June 6 with a predawn airborne drop of 24,000 British and American paratroopers behind the beach designated "Utah," near the city of Caen. Although many paratroopers were accidentally dropped far from their objectives, they still caused great confusion behind the lines, and their 15 percent casualty rate was lower than some experts had predicted after the Sicily disasters.

After an air and naval bombardment, Bradley's infantry landed at 6:30 a.m. on Omaha and Utah beaches. The 23,000 men of the Fourth Division assaulting Utah Beach faced relatively calm surf and an enemy division of reservists and foreign volunteers who quickly surrendered after close combat. In addition, a lucky accident placed the division on the wrong beach, out of range of the heaviest enemy artillery. The Fourth quickly pushed six miles inland, receiving only 197 casualties.

Unlike Utah, Omaha Beach was a nightmare, with waves three to six feet high, making the soldiers cold, wet, and seasick. The surf swamped the special amphibious Sherman tanks meant to provide artillery support. Facing steel and concrete underwater obstacles, mines, a low sea wall, sand dunes, and bluffs, and with little cover, the Fifth Corps had to fight two regiments of German troops, including the tough 352nd Division, which had arrived near the beach on maneuvers only shortly before the invasion. By noon, the Allied forces had only taken about ten yards of beach, but they forced their way up the bluffs over the next two hours with the help of U.S. Navy gunners, losing about 2,500 men during the ascent.

The British fared better on Gold, Juno, and Sword beaches: they had only 1,300 casualties. Meanwhile, the deception that Pas de Calais would be the site of the invasion worked. Hitler's staff would not release the twenty-four divisions waiting for Patton's fake invasion and would not let two panzer divisions near Chartres move toward Caen as requested by the German commander, Field Marshal Gerd von Rundstedt, until late in the afternoon. The German counterattack arrived too late to stop the Allied invasion but early enough to keep Montgomery's forces from taking Caen.

Although the D-day invasion was successful overall, Bradley and Eisenhower grew impatient at Montgomery's inability to take Caen on D-day or soon after. Not taking Caen weakened the left flank of the invasion and made it difficult for the air forces, which needed the city's airfields. Once again, his troops plodded along too slowly; even his communications were slow. Eisenhower criticized Bradley for not sending him enough progress reports on D-day, but Bradley learned all the messages he had sent were lost in Montgomery's cipher room, which was running twelve hours behind.

Repeatedly delaying his offensive until he could build up more provisions, the British general's slow pace made it essential that Bradley take Cherbourg, so the Allies would have more port facilities to ship in supplies. Montgomery finally moved on June 25 and failed to take Caen again. Bradley took Cherbourg and the Contentin Peninsula the next day.

The Allies had to break out of Normandy or risk allowing the situation to devolve into a stalemate. Bradley first tried an attack across a wide front, which proved unsuccessful, and then formulated Operation Cobra, an assault on a very narrow front near St. Lô. Not to be outdone, Montgomery devised Operation Goodwood, a supposedly limited offensive launched two days before Cobra and designed to take pressure off Bradley.

Operation Goodwood failed. Montgomery was only able to gain the rest of Caen and about six miles to the south at a cost of 4,000 casualties and one-third of his tanks. Eisenhower wanted to relieve Montgomery, but the British would not permit it. Meanwhile, in Germany, Hitler's generals tried to assassinate him, and the German general staff was in disarray. If Bradley's Cobra operation did not succeed, the Allied general staff might find itself in similar straits.

Operation Cobra opened July 25 with an aerial bombardment. Unfortunately, the bombardment accidentally killed and wounded hundreds of Americans. But it also killed more than 1,000 Germans. Bradley's Seventh Corps under Joe Collins was able to storm through the hole blown in the lines by the bombardment, and Bradley pushed through more tanks and men behind Collins. His army had finally broken through, and his tanks pushed through to Avranches at the base of the Brittany peninsula.

On August 1, Bradley became commander of the Twelfth Army Group, which meant turning over control of the First Army to General Courtney Hodges and activating the Third Army under George Patton. As commander of most of the American infantry forces in Europe, Bradley was promoted to permanent major general and was officially on the same level as Montgomery, although Monty would keep pushing to regain his status as overall ground commander until the end of the war.

After seizing Avranches, Bradley sent Patton's tanks blazing into the Brittany peninsula in an effort to gain more ports. At that time, all supplies had to move through Cherbourg and the Normandy beaches, which were frequently closed due to bad weather. The Germans countered, however, by withdrawing and holding the Brittany ports tightly until they were of little use to the Allies. Bradley's forces pushed forward through Normandy.

Soon Bradley faced a new opportunity to trap the Germans. In the original Overlord plan, the Allied forces had assumed that Hitler would gradually withdraw and force a showdown battle closer to Germany, but Ultra and information from captured POWs showed that Hitler had forbidden any withdrawal and was in fact reinforcing his troops in Normandy. This tactical mistake gave the Allies a chance to surround the Germans and ultimately win the war. Bradley began drawing up plans.

Hitler ordered his commander in the area, Guenther von Kluge, to counterattack at Mortain, which lay on the hinge between two major Allied salients, located roughly due east of the Normandy and Brittany peninsulas. Ultra intelligence gave little warning until the night before the attack, but Bradley quickly moved more men into the area to meet it. After the attack began, Ultra showed that the Mortain offensive was a major offensive and not just a bluff to cover a withdrawal as Bradley first suspected.

A major offensive meant Hitler had committed an even greater tactical blunder. If Montgomery's Canadians could push southeastward through the town of Falaise and beyond to Argentan, and if Bradley's American forces could push northward, the two armies could meet in Argentan, surround and trap the Germans, and possibly win the war within days.

Of course, for the maneuver to work, Montgomery's army would have to reach Argentan. Bradley's forces made it, but, once again, Montgomery's troops failed to reach their objective. Realizing the trap's jaws were closing, the Germans counterattacked Bradley's forces to fight their way out. When they saw that Montgomery's troops had not shut the door, they escaped through the Falaise Gap. Montgomery finally took Falaise seventy-one days after D-day. The Allied armies regrouped and tried to trap the Germans again farther east, but they did not have enough strength to stop the enemy from breaking through to safety beyond the Seine River.

The Allies had won a great victory in Normandy. But Bradley admitted in retrospect that he and the other Allied generals should have learned from Hitler's Mortain offensive that the Führer was not a conventional military thinker and that he was taking desperate chances. Had they taken the example to heart, they might have been more prepared for Hitler's later Ardennes offensive in the Battle of the Bulge.

Bradley's armies chased the Germans across France. The enemy was in full retreat, except for pockets of stubborn resistance in the Brittany ports. Brest held out for another month. Soon after the Allies landed troops in southern France, near Marseilles, the country was fully liberated. Originally, the Allies planned to bypass Paris, but a spontaneous uprising on August 19, 1944, by the French Resistance changed their plans. Bradley detoured his Fifth Corps under General Gee Gerow to take Paris and join French general Jacques LeClerc, going in first, and General Charles DeGaulle leading a parade down the Champs-Elysées.

With the conquest of Germany looming, Bradley grappled with Montgomery over strategy. Eisenhower mediated. Montgomery pushed to lead a single thrust into the heart of Germany from the north. In return, Patton suggested a single thrust to the south, under his command, but Bradley overruled that. Bradley preferred a two-pronged attack on Germany as originally agreed. Eisenhower decided to stick to the original double-thrust idea, but he allowed Montgomery a larger force, giving Bradley's First Army to the British general so he could move faster to take Antwerp, an important port through which supplies could flow.

By late August, Bradley's forces under Patton and Hodges had advanced nearly to the German border. Montgomery's drive was equally successful, advancing 250 miles in six days and liberating Amiens, Lille, Brussels, and the Antwerp docks. But then Montgomery blundered twice. Instead of pushing on to cross the Rhine River, seventy-five miles away, he halted and missed his chance. Then he failed to fully capture Antwerp, which meant Bradley's forces would be short of supplies.

To gain full use of Antwerp's port, the U.S. Navy warned Montgomery that he needed to clear the Schelde estuary, a sixty-mile channel between Antwerp's docks and the open sea, and the German batteries on islands adjacent to the Schelde. Otherwise, the German guns would prevent ships from reaching the docks. Montgomery failed to take the guns, and the Germans reinforced them. What might have been a quick and easy job turned into a major campaign to remove the enemy, and Antwerp's port was not available for three months. Now short on gasoline and ammunition, Bradley had to stop Hodges's army north of the Ardennes forest, ten miles east of the German border. Meeting fierce resistance, and literally running out of gas, Patton's advance also slowed to a crawl.

Bradley was less than pleased with Montgomery's results. Then, when the first German V-2 rockets hit London on September 8, Montgomery devised Operation Market Garden, a plan for an operation during which he would land airborne troops along the road that traversed the Netherlands all the way to the Rhine River. Bradley protested the foolhardy idea, suggesting that Montgomery should focus on opening Antwerp instead. Bradley suspected Montgomery was using Market Garden as a springboard to unilaterally launch his single thrust plan into Germany. Eisenhower approved the operation for three reasons: to get Montgomery moving, to use the airborne forces, and to capture the V-2 rocket sites. As author Cornelius Ryan described in the book *A Bridge Too Far,* when the operation finally launched after several delays, Market Garden turned into a disaster. Seventeen thousand men were reported killed, wounded, or missing. In addition, the operation diverted attention from the opening of Antwerp and slowed the advance into Germany by diverting supplies that might have allowed Bradley's forces to reach the Rhine before the Germans could regroup.

The advance into Germany would be nothing like the dash across France. Eisenhower held to his plan to let Montgomery have a relatively "full-blooded" thrust into Germany and ordered Bradley to slow Patton's advance. But Montgomery's big offensive never got going due to his own mistakes. He first criticized Eisenhower's leadership to George Marshall and then took another three weeks to open Antwerp, at a cost of 13,000 lives. Having enough of him, Eisenhower decided to forgo the British commander's plan and followed Bradley's two-pronged strategy instead.

In November, Bradley's forces reached the Saar and Roer rivers but could not push through into Germany. German resistance had stiffened, but the Allies believed the Germans would soon collapse under the weight of their huge losses on the eastern front and the constant bombing of German cities. None of the Allied commanders thought Hitler would, or could, mount a major assault.

Ultra intelligence did not warn of an upcoming German offensive. Hitler had ordered complete radio silence, and Bradley and his staff thought the logical time and place for Hitler to counterattack was after the Allies had crossed the Roer River, where the terrain was good for tanks. Gambling that Hitler would not be stupid enough to attack through the Ardennes forest, Bradley manned it thinly with inexperienced troops. Even if the Germans mounted an attack there and pushed forward, he thought, it could be beaten with a pincers movement from north and south of any resulting salient.

When Hitler's tanks and men poured through the Allied lines at five different points in the Ardennes to begin the Battle of the Bulge on December 16, 1944, Bradley at first believed the Germans had launched a limited attack to stop the American armies from moving farther into Germany. Ultra soon confirmed the attack was much larger. Bradley ordered Hodges and Patton to attack in pincer fashion on both sides of the expanding bulge formed by the German troops, with the intent of trapping the enemy between them.

Some historians have been critical of Bradley's handling of the Battle of the Bulge. Jerry Morelock said that Bradley "provided inferior leadership during the Battle of the Bulge," that he was "caught with his pants down," and that he had "lost touch with the situation." Other historians, such as Charles B. McDonald in *A Time for Trumpets,* note the general consensus among U.S. intelligence experts that Hitler would not make such a stupid gamble of all his resources on a last-ditch offensive. It is clear that the entire U.S. Army, not just Bradley, thought such an attack unlikely.

Regardless, the final result, after weeks of hard fighting, was a win for the Allies. Hitler's gamble wasted men and materiel that could have been used to prolong the war. Like Grant at Shiloh, Bradley recovered from a desperate situation and turned the tables on the enemy. Patton worked closely with Bradley to defeat the German drive, attacking northward with three divisions to relieve the Americans surrounded in the town of Bastogne. Hodges and his corps commanders also regrouped, and after a few days it was clear the German offensive would eventually wither and die.

While American men were fighting in the Ardennes, Montgomery maneuvered, using the Bulge as his latest excuse to revive his one-thrust strategy. Arguing that the forces on the north and south shoulders of the bulge would have difficulty communicating with each other, he convinced Eisenhower to temporarily give him command of Bradley's northern units. Once in command of more Americans, Montgomery's meddling almost resulted in lengthening the war by ordering Hodges to give up territory and by not allowing him to attack the waist of the bulge. Instead, the British general wanted to retreat and regroup. When Hodges balked, Montgomery tried to get him relieved of command.

On December 23, good weather made Patton's advance on Bastogne easier and allowed fighters and bombers to begin hitting the Germans. If Montgomery had allowed Hodges to attack, he might have met up with Patton and trapped the Germans in a vise, as Bradley had wanted to do earlier at the Falaise Gap. It would be the turning point in the Battle of the Bulge, if Montgomery could be convinced to move.

But Montgomery was convinced that Hodges would not be able to mount an offensive for three months, that Patton's advance would not work, and that the Allies should go on the defensive until he could mount his plan for a single thrust into Berlin. But Ultra showed Bradley that Hitler's offensive was failing, and now was the time to attack. Patton broke through to Bastogne on December 26, and General Joe Collins, disregarding Montgomery's orders, attacked and destroyed the Second German Panzer division.

Bradley urged Eisenhower to approve the pincer attack on the waist of the bulge at once and, assuming they could trap Hitler's army, suggested it be followed by a "hurry-up" thrust through the center of the line. Eisenhower approved the operation because he thought the maneuver might bring all the Allied forces to the Rhine before launching the final push into Germany. Although still stalling the start of his colossal northern offensive, Montgomery told Eisenhower that he did not like Bradley's hurry-up operation or Eisenhower's overall broad-front strategy. He wrote a letter demanding that it be cancelled and that all of Bradley's armies be placed under his command. Only when Eisenhower threatened to resign did Montgomery back down.

On January 3, 1945, the British general finally let his American troops attack the north shoulder of the Bulge. The two Allied pincers met January 16 at Houffalize, but it was too late to trap most of the Germans, who had escaped again as they had at the Falaise Gap. Eisenhower then ordered Bradley's offensive to commence, giving it precedence over Montgomery's thrust into Germany. But when Bradley was slowed down by bad weather, Eisenhower halted his forces after several days so Montgomery could launch his grand offensive.

Montgomery's thrust to the Rhine was to proceed in three stages. Hodges would seize the Roer Dams, the British and Canadian forces would attack southeast from Nijmegen in the Netherlands, and the American Ninth Army under General William Simpson would attack northeastward to the Rhine. While Montgomery's offensive was running, Bradley was forced to order Patton to maintain merely an "aggressive defense."

The operation against the Roer Dams failed. U.S. troops broke through, but not before German engineers blew up the dams, flooding the Roer Valley, delaying Simpson's crossing for two weeks, and bogging down the second stage of the operation in the mud. On February 23, General Simpson finally crossed the Roer, and moved to the Rhine River, capturing 52,000 German soldiers, and linking up with the British and Canadian forces. He asked to cross the Rhine, but Montgomery would not let him. Bradley brought his forces to the Rhine by March 7, where they waited for Montgomery's huge Operation Plunder to charge into the heart of Germany on March 24.

Bradley let Patton advance south across the Moselle River in a major offensive to trap the Germans between two major American forces. They hoped it might develop into their own thrust into Germany, but it would have to happen by accident to avoid Montgomery's interference. The lucky accident arrived on Hodges's front instead. On March 7, 1945, Hodges phoned Bradley saying the Ninth Armored Division had captured the railway bridge over the Rhine at Remagen. The Germans had tried to blow it up along with all the other bridges but had failed. Now Bradley could return to the original idea of the two-thrust attack into Germany if Eisenhower approved his plan. Eisenhower told Bradley to put everything across that he could. The Germans did all they could to stop the beachhead, even firing eleven V-2 rockets at the bridge, which eventually collapsed.

But Bradley's bridgehead was secure. Slowly, his forces enlarged it, preparing for a breakout to the southeast. Patton quickly advanced and crossed the Rhine on March 23. Bradley held a news conference to make sure the American media knew that both Patton and Hodges were across before Montgomery's operation began. Montgomery's huge Rhine crossing commenced the following day, and the Germans were soon overrun. Bradley then ordered Hodges to break out of the Remagen bridgehead and Patton to push for Frankfurt. Eisenhower ordered more troops and supplies for Bradley's southern thrust, and the British were forced to agree that Bradley and Eisenhower had proved correct in their original pursuit of a two-pronged strategy.

The time had come to implement the final conquest of Germany. Although Eisenhower, Bradley, Patton, and Hodges all had a hand in devising the plan, it became known as the Bradley plan. The British did not like the plan, and it grew controversial in light of later Cold War developments, but it offered a way to link up with the Russians. Bradley and Eisenhower decided not to push for Berlin, a move that would not have furthered their objectives, and they agreed that U.S. troops should stop at the line formed by the Elbe and Mulde rivers. The Russians were already within thirty-five miles of Berlin, and it would be in Russian hands long before U.S. troops could get there. Besides, the Allied political leaders had already decided on the zones of occupation, so even if the American forces took territory on the way to Berlin, they would just have to hand it over to the Russians later. It was more important for the Allies to link up without accidentally firing on each other.

Winston Churchill complained when Eisenhower notified Stalin of the linkup plans. Concerned with postwar politics, the British prime minister wanted to head for Berlin, partly because the Russians were already violating their agreements to hold free elections in their conquered territories. Eisenhower patiently explained the military reasons behind the Bradley plan, Marshall backed him, and the American generals prevailed.

The Bradley plan also included procedures to deal with possible Nazi redoubts, a threat based on intelligence reports that Hitler, top Nazis, and fanatical SS troops would make a final stand in the Austrian Alps or in Norway's mountains. Therefore, the Allies decided to push southeastward to cut off escape to the Alps and northeastward to seal off Denmark, which provided the most practical route to Norway. Tactically, the Bradley plan meant surrounding German forces in the Ruhr industrial area, driving across central Germany, and halting at the Elbe to meet the Russians. Eisenhower returned the U.S. Ninth Army to Bradley for the main push across Germany, infuriating Montgomery and his friends in London. But Eisenhower was beyond caring about Montgomery's demands.

By Easter Day, April 1, Generals Simpson and Collins encircled the Ruhr, and 317,000 Germans surrendered. Another 70,000 Germans soon surrendered in the Harz Mountains. The Americans reached the Elbe in less than two weeks. In the north, Montgomery took his time cutting off the Danish border, and Bradley believed his British counterpart had lost all heart for the fight after being denied the glory of taking Berlin. Eventually, Eisenhower grew concerned the Russians might take Denmark, so he ordered Montgomery to accept help from U.S. general Matt Ridgway, who sped 250 miles from the Ruhr to the Elbe in three days, sealing off Denmark and capturing 510,000 Germans on the way.

Simpson or Patton could have been sent on to Berlin, but there was no gasoline supply system yet beyond the Elbe. Like Churchill, Patton wanted to take Berlin because he distrusted the Russians, but Bradley and Eisenhower said no. Bradley sent Patton southward to prevent any chance of an Alpine redoubt.

On April 12, Bradley heard the news that President Roosevelt had died. Four days later, the Russians surrounded Berlin and closed in on its center. One hundred thousand Russians and many Germans died in the assault. On April 30, Hitler and his wife, Eva Braun, committed suicide.

The Russian linkup occurred April 26. Having reached the Danube, Patton pressured Bradley and Eisenhower to let him take Prague, but Eisenhower refused. On May 7, the Germans surrendered, and the war in Europe ended at one minute after midnight, May 9, 1945.

Although willing to join MacArthur in the Pacific, Bradley would have had to take a demotion to do so. In November, President Harry S. Truman named Marshall special emissary to China and chose Eisenhower for army chief of staff. Eisenhower told Bradley he would be in line for the job next, but Bradley's first responsibility would be to tackle the Veterans Administration (VA), which was under attack for mismanagement.

After a quick victory tour back home and a month as acting commander in Europe, Bradley met with Eisenhower and President Truman at the Potsdam Conference on July 17, 1945. In his memoirs, Bradley said the president discussed with the two generals domestic and international politics and the possibile use of the atomic bomb, which would soon be dropped on Hiroshima and Nagasaki. After the conference, Bradley left Europe for good and began his job as the director of the Veterans Administration on August 15, the day after Japan surrendered.

Drastic reforms were needed at the Veterans Administration, which had been established in 1930 to consolidate all federal services for veterans. Now the United States had four times as many veterans as before the war. The GI Bill of Rights had recently been enacted, and the number of students in colleges and universities quickly rose to twice its prewar level. Disability claims skyrocketed from an expected 60,000 to 400,000 applications a month. There were 200,000 home loans to guarantee and 175 million new insurance policies to administer. Millions of inbound letters from veterans and outbound premium notices had to be handled by clerks faced with such problems as which "Bill Kelly" from the 28,000 William Kellys in the files had sent the latest letter. Bradley decentralized the agency, creating 13 branch offices and adding 7,000 personnel. He created 1,000 rating boards to review insurance claims and reformed VA education programs.

The biggest challenge came in improving medical care. To attract more talented doctors, Bradley took the VA hospitals out of the civil service and linked them with the best medical schools around the country. When congressmen and bureaucrats fought the changes, Bradley threatened to resign. Although he initially had not wanted the job, Bradley was later very proud of his VA service.

Meanwhile, he watched a new world order evolve, with Patton's December 1945 death in an auto accident symbolizing the end of the old order. Bradley saw the draft expire, the army shrink from 8.2 million to less than a million, and President Truman integrate the armed forces by executive order in July 1947. He also watched Eisenhower and Truman develop a unified structure for the armed forces. After much debate and military infighting, Congress approved the National Security Act, which Truman signed on July 26, 1947, creating the National Military Establishment with a secretary of defense presiding over three coequal services: the army, the navy, and the air force—each with its own civilian secretary. The landmark legislation gave the Joint Chiefs of Staff legal standing and created the National Security Council (NSC) and the Central Intelligence Agency (CIA).

Promoted to permanent four-star general, Bradley took over as army chief of staff in February 1948. Slowly, it became clear that the United States was embroiled in a long-term struggle, the "Cold War" against communism and the Soviet Union. Bradley helped gradually formulate a policy in which the United States and its allies would contain Soviet expansion by giving aid to anticommunist governments around the world. Bradley worked with the other two chiefs, Admiral Louis E. Denfeld and General Carl Spatz, to work out the military implications of containment. Although getting tough with the Russians logically called for a military buildup, defense spending had actually shrunk due to the changing economic and political climate.

A year earlier, while Bradley was still revamping the VA, the president had decided that funds were needed to fight communism in Europe, including $400 million in Truman Doctrine funds to fight insurgents in Greece and Turkey and a $17 billion Marshall Plan aid package, named for now Secretary of State George Marshall, to rebuild Europe's shattered economy.

Within weeks of becoming army chief of staff, Bradley had to respond to the Soviet Union's overthrowing of the government of Czechoslovakia and the Berlin Blockade crisis, during which the Soviets cut off Allied ground and railroad access to West Berlin, and shut off its electricity. While needing to assert Allied right of access, Bradley and the administration did not want to start a shooting war. Bradley's Joint Chiefs eventually decided to employ the Berlin Airlift, an around-the-clock Allied supply effort using every air transport plane available, to break the blockade.

While helping the administration define its overall policy of containment, Bradley worked to refine the basic contingency plan for a war with the Soviet Union, known as massive retaliation, which was based on America's atomic monopoly. The Joint Chiefs assumed the Soviets would overrun Western Europe with their larger numbers of soldiers and tanks. Nine days later, the U.S. would drop atomic bombs on them, and then occupy Western Europe and Russia. Bradley's Joint Chiefs modified this strategy to include a defensive stand at the Rhine River in the first formal document outlining containment policy, National Security Council Paper Number 20/4 on November 24, 1948.

Containment policy evolved over time and grew to include collective security. The North Atlantic Treaty was signed on April 4, 1949, establishing the North Atlantic Treaty Organization (NATO). Truman made Eisenhower the NATO supreme commander, ignoring opposition from Old Guard Republicans and conservative Democrats who wanted to return to the isolationist policies of the past.

On August 16, 1949, Bradley was sworn in as the first chairman of the Joint Chiefs of Staff. Earlier in the year, the National Security

Act had renamed the National Military Establishment the "Department of Defense" and created the chairman position.

Because funds were tight, the three branches of the armed services fought openly over their budgets. The navy had based its future on a new supercarrier, but the new defense secretary, Louis Johnson, killed it. This action led to an "Admirals Revolt" in which navy officers leaked a document accusing administration officials of receiving kickbacks on the procurement of the air force's B-36 bomber, which the memo also labeled a "billion dollar blunder." In testimony before the House Armed Services committee hearings on the issue, Bradley attacked the navy's political tactics, calling the admirals "fancy Dans," who refused to play for the good of the whole team unless they called all the signals.

Bradley had to restore the team spirit within the military, and it became clear that a new game plan was needed. On August 29, 1949, the Soviets exploded their own atomic bomb, ending U.S. nuclear monopoly. Truman approved increased production of nuclear bombs, and Bradley's Joint Chiefs helped convince the president to pursue the hydrogen bomb, which was a thousand times more powerful. It was tested in 1952, followed less than a year later by the Russians testing their own.

While avoiding war in Europe and coping with the arms race, Bradley's Joint Chiefs also had to deal with events in the Far East. Defeating Chiang Kai-Shek's nationalists after a long civil war, Chinese communists declared the People's Republic of China on October 1, 1949, and the nationalists fled to Formosa. The Russian bomb and the fall of China's national government led to the defining National Security Council Cold War document, NSC-68, in April 1950, which said the United States should spend three times more on its military. Another document in July 1951 warned that the Soviets would manufacture 200 atomic bombs within two years, a move that would require the U.S. to step up production and expand its military.

Clearly, the U.S. also would have to contain communism in Asia. Bradley met with General MacArthur, the commander in the Far East, and they decided that Formosa, Japan, and the Ryukyu Islands were important for the U.S. defensive perimeter in the Pacific, while

General Bradley meeting with General Douglas MacArthur at Haneda Air Force Base in Japan, June 23, 1950. Best known for his role in World War II, Bradley also helped develop the military infrastructure to fight the Cold War. (U.S. Army Photograph, courtesy State Historical Society of Missouri, Columbia.)

Korea was not. The U.S. decided to provide only a handful of military advisors to Korea, a Japanese colony for forty years that had been divided by agreement at the 38th parallel between a Communist North and a capitalist South, with national elections and unification expected in the near future.

A United Press reporter woke Bradley at 10 p.m. on June 24, 1950, asking about North Korea's invasion of South Korea. Within days, it became clear that the South Korean Army could not repel the invasion on its own. The Truman administration decided it had to resist the attack or other countries in Asia might also fall to the Communists.

United Nations commander Douglas MacArthur pushed for more troops and wanted to accept troops offered by Taiwan. Truman approved two more divisions for Korea and a naval blockade of

North Korea, but he declined to use the Chinese nationalist forces. Truman distrusted MacArthur. He was an ally of the president's political enemies and tended to take action on his own without authorization. For military advice, Truman turned to Bradley and Marshall, and he soon asked Marshall to be his secretary of defense.

By early August, 50,000 U.S. troops were fighting under the United Nations banner alongside 45,000 South Korean forces, but the United Nations forces were losing, and being pushed south to a perimeter around the city of Pusan. MacArthur proposed landing U.S. forces at Inchon on the west coast of Korea to outflank the North Koreans, a move the Japanese had used in the Russo-Japanese War. The Joint Chiefs approved the plan but thought it risky. They asked MacArthur repeatedly for detailed invasion plans, but he slyly told the Joint Chiefs that he would send the plans by courier on September 5 to arrive in Washington six days later. The courier did not arrive until 11 p.m. September 13, and he briefed the Joint Chiefs at 11 a.m. the next morning, six and a half hours before the September 15 invasion began.

Bradley began to distrust MacArthur as well, especially when the general began to engage in his own diplomacy. The Joint Chiefs ordered him not to visit Formosa, but he went anyway, telling former nationalist president Chiang Kai-Shek he would send Taiwan U.S. jet fighters, which he was not authorized to do. Not wanting to start a war with Red China over Taiwan, Truman told MacArthur to stop playing diplomat and made it clear that no U.S. forces would be placed on Formosa without his permission.

When MacArthur denounced administration policy in a speech to the Veterans of Foreign Wars, Truman ordered the general to withdraw the statement publicly, and he considered replacing him with Bradley, who had recently been promoted to five-star General of the Army, the last of the World War II generals to receive the honor.

Bradley began to see a pattern of insubordination developing in MacArthur's actions, but he had to admire MacArthur's results. His Inchon landing was a huge success. It took the North Koreans by surprise, and he was deemed a military genius by the press. MacArthur's forces then chased the enemy northward. Instead of continuing up the peninsula, however, MacArthur decided to launch another amphibious assault on the port city of Wonsan to gain a port for supplies. This maneuver wasted time: it slowed down the U.S. offensive and allowed the North Koreans to regroup. In addition, the harbor turned out to be too heavily mined to be of use.

Bradley and the Joint Chiefs did not want the conflict to escalate into full-scale war with Korea's neighbors, Russia and China. The Joint Chiefs ordered MacArthur to destroy the North Korean forces, but he was to do nothing to cause Soviet or Chinese intervention, such as placing U.S. troops in provinces along the northern border or moving forces into Chinese or Soviet territory.

Even with diplomatic warnings from China and mounting evidence that Chinese troops were massing in Manchuria, the U.S. administration, the Joint Chiefs, Bradley, and MacArthur all thought that the Chinese were bluffing, that the Russians would not risk global war, and that it was too late for a Chinese intervention to make a difference in Korea.

On October 9, MacArthur issued an ultimatum, demanding that the North Koreans surrender. China and North Korea rejected the demand. Within a week, 180,000 Chinese troops began secretly crossing the Yalu River into Korea. To calm administration fears about the Chinese, MacArthur told Truman and Bradley that North Korean resistance would end by Thanksgiving, predicting U.S. troops would be withdrawn by Christmas and Korean elections would occur by the first of the year.

On October 24, without authorization, MacArthur ordered U.S. units to drive toward Korea's northern border. The Chinese attacked two days later, and the U.S. victory in Korea quickly turned into defeat. It became clear to Bradley in the coming weeks that MacArthur faced a much greater threat than first thought, 300,000 Chinese rather than his estimated 25,000, and the Joint Chiefs began looking for alternate strategies and commanders. But MacArthur announced publicly that he would bring the boys home by Christmas, a prediction that Bradley saw as foolish.

On November 25, the Chinese ambushed U.S. forces and nearly surrounded them. Finally, MacArthur had to admit he was in trouble, and his frantic messages made Bradley think the aging general had lost his nerve. To turn the situation around, the Joint Chiefs sent General

Matt Ridgway to command the ground troops in Korea while MacArthur maintained overall command. Under Ridgway, the military situation stabilized into a stalemate, with Chinese offensives and American counteroffensives moving back and forth across the peninsula.

Bradley looked on as MacArthur continued to publicly attack administration policy in the media, accusing Truman of keeping him from finishing off the North Koreans and painting U.S. allies as shortsighted and selfish. Almost relieving MacArthur then, Truman decided instead to issue an executive order allowing no government employee to make public statements about policy without clearance from the White House.

Truman decided not to leave Korea voluntarily but to push diplomatically for an armistice at the 38th parallel. The president told MacArthur that he planned to send a peace message to China. But MacArthur would not cooperate, and Bradley and the Joint Chiefs worried that he might propel the U.S. into war with China and the Soviet Union. Soon MacArthur made his move. Desperately wanting the Republicans to defeat Truman in the 1952 presidential election, preferably with his name on the ticket, MacArthur released a statement to the Chinese Communists mocking Truman's policies, ridiculing Chinese soldiers, and threatening to widen the war. He upstaged the president's peace message and implied that the Chinese should come to MacArthur personally to pursue a peace agreement.

When Truman reminded MacArthur of his executive order forbidding foreign policy statements, the general attacked the president in a letter to a congressman and in a right-wing magazine, *The Freeman*. Bradley conferred with the Joint Chiefs, and with Truman and Marshall, to decide what to do about MacArthur. Relieving the general would result in fresh attacks on Marshall and Bradley, who might even be seen as exacting Pershing's last revenge; nevertheless, Bradley and the Joint Chiefs decided to relieve MacArthur because of his continuing negative public statements which were at odds with the administration and its policies and because of the need to maintain civilian control over the military. Truman and his advisors agreed with Bradley and named Ridgway to replace MacArthur. Because a newspaper got wind of the story, Truman announced MacArthur's firing during a news conference at 1 a.m. on April 11,

1951. Radio reports about his dismissal reached Tokyo before the Joint Chiefs could reach MacArthur.

Truman delivered the news to the public during a speech to the nation the next day, but many still considered the general a hero. Five days later, MacArthur returned to the United States in triumph, the same day Bradley gave a speech that was seen as a public rebuttal of MacArthur. Bradley then became a prime target, as Marshall already was, for MacArthur's right-wing friends. On April 19, MacArthur spoke before a joint session of Congress and delivered his memorable line, "Old soldiers never die; they just fade away," which brought him even more public acclaim. The Korean War would end only after two more years of bloody combat, with both sides recognizing that they had reached a stalemate and signing an armistice dividing Korea at the 38th Parallel.

Bradley watched the Truman-MacArthur feud play out in the political arena as the parties worked to secure the top generals as candidates. Although Truman had wanted Eisenhower for the Democratic presidential ticket, he ran on the Republican ticket, becoming with Senator Robert Taft, who was known as "Mr. Republican," a prime candidate for the Republican nomination in 1952. Taft had voted against NATO, but Eisenhower, like Bradley, believed alliances such as NATO were necessary to meet the Communist threat. He offered Taft a deal. If Taft would support NATO, Eisenhower would back out and support Taft in the presidential race. Taft refused, and Eisenhower got the nomination. Taft had selected MacArthur as his running mate and had Eisenhower not won, the fired general might have become president in mid-1953 when Taft died of cancer.

During the campaign, Taft had promised to fire Bradley if elected. Truman and Eisenhower defended Bradley, who responded by speaking out against isolationism as selfish and defensive. Bradley said that U.S. security needed a forward-based strategy employing collective arrangements with other nations.

Bradley thought it fortunate that Eisenhower, MacArthur's former aide and speechwriter, finally buried MacArthur's political career. But he was dismayed when Eisenhower's alliance with the Republicans led his colleague to attack the friends and policies he

Bradley ranked forty-fourth in the West Point class of 1915. While first in his class to receive the ranks of brigadier and lieutenant general (first and third stars), he was the second to reach major general (second star) after Air Corps general Joseph T. McNarney. (Missouri State Archives.)

had helped shape. As Bradley saw it, Eisenhower sold out his principles and friendships to become president. Truman, also deeply hurt by the campaign, said he should have groomed Bradley for the presidency instead. While flattered, Bradley did not want the job.

During the campaign, Eisenhower stood on a platform supporting Senator William Jenner, who had called George Marshall a "living lie." At the request of Senator Joseph McCarthy, who had also attacked Marshall in public, Eisenhower agreed to delete text that praised Marshall from a speech he planned to give. And Eisenhower publicly blamed Truman for the Korean War, implying he could win it simply by "going to Korea."

As promised, President Eisenhower traveled to Korea, taking Bradley with him. Bradley briefed the new president about recent atomic weapons improvements and about the recent successful test of the first hydrogen bomb. He asked Eisenhower not to politicize the Joint Chiefs by replacing them all at once, suggesting he let attrition do the job. Bradley and the other chiefs would leave within a year or so anyway. Under Eisenhower, the only real policy change Bradley noticed was a more aggressive stance against the Chinese in March 1953, when the president and Secretary of State John Foster Dulles threatened to use nuclear weapons and widen the war beyond Korea if the Chinese and North Koreans did not begin peace talks. Talks resumed on April 26, three months before the July 27 armistice.

Bradley stepped down as chairman of the Joint Chiefs of Staff in August 1953 at the age of sixty. He lived twenty-eight more years, moving to the Los Angeles area and serving as chairman of the board of the Bulova Watch Company until 1973. When his son-in-law died in a 1954 jet fighter crash, his daughter and four grandchildren moved in with him. Within a few years, his daughter remarried, moved to the Washington, D.C., area, and had two more children. The Bradleys soon moved back to Washington as well. Bradley's first wife died in 1965, and he soon married a Hollywood screenwriter, Kitty Buhler, who was twenty-nine years younger than he. They visited Vietnam in 1967 and then moved to Beverly Hills in 1968. Bradley and his wife served as advisors on the movie *Patton*.

In 1973, at the age of eighty, blood clots in his lungs nearly killed Bradley. Clots in his brain threatened his life two years later, and he moved into an army extensive care facility at Fort Bliss in El Paso, Texas. On April 8, 1981, as he was being wheeled into an elevator, Omar Bradley died instantly of a brain clot. He was eighty-eight. Six days later, Air Force One carried his body to Washington, D.C., for burial in Arlington National Cemetery.

Although he was most famous for his World War II exploits, Bradley's role in shaping national defense to face the challenges of the Cold War may have been his most important achievement. His emphasis on education and training, as both teacher and student, promoted the growth of professionalism and management skills within the U.S. Army, an important factor in the reorganization and modernization of the armed forces to face the Soviet threat.

For more reading

Bradley, by Charles Whiting (New York: Ballantine Books, 1971), is a quick read that gives a decent overview of Omar Bradley's career. It strongly questions his generalship during the Battle of the Bulge with little documentation.

A General's Life, by Omar N. Bradley and Clay Blair (New York: Simon and Schuster, 1983), is the definitive autobiography of Bradley's life and career.

A Soldier's Story, by Omar N. Bradley (New York: Random House, 1999), is a good autobiographical account of his role in World War II, but it does not delve deeply into his life.

7

Conclusion

Former University of Missouri–Columbia chancellor Haskell Monroe once observed that Missouri does not know to which section of the country it belongs. It is at the same time eastern, western, northern, and southern. As the nation's crossroads for much of its history, Missouri attracted travelers and settlers from many parts of the world, many of whom had an impact on the state's development. Because of the diversity of its people, the state provides a microcosm of the rest of America, and the lives of Missouri generals tend to reflect the rest of America as well. Perhaps this is one reason Missouri has produced so many interesting military leaders.

Interestingly, the top Missouri generals tended to be men of peace for the most part, only turning to war when they felt it absolutely necessary. When possible, they relied on diplomacy first, as Doniphan did with the Mormons and Navajos, as Pershing did with the Moro tribesmen in the Philippines, and as both Doniphan and Price did in trying to avoid civil war. They were wise enough to understand that it was usually better to achieve one's objective via a handshake than at the point of a bayonet.

In studying the lives of these generals and the wars in which they fought, it is clear that the origins of one war usually lie in a previous conflict. The War of 1812 with Britain was fought to determine unresolved issues remaining from the American Revolution. Ulysses

S. Grant wrote in his memoirs that the seeds of the Civil War were planted during the Mexican War. The Nazis launched World War II to avenge Germany's defeat in World War I and the severity of the terms imposed by the victors in the Treaty of Versailles, which in turn was the result of many earlier European conflicts and rivalries. The Vietnam War was a continuation of the revolt against the French in Indochina, and it was also one in a string of Cold War conflicts between the United States and Soviet Union, each of which led to the next. The war in Iraq was launched to resolve issues from the Gulf War, in turn an outgrowth of the Cold War.

The careers of the generals show that it has been important for each generation of military leadership to pass on its lessons to the next. Although the later war is rarely anything like the previous one, the lessons must still be learned and applied in a different context. The generals of World War II took lessons from World War I, particularly in trying to avoid the static trench warfare of earlier conflicts. Relying on the earlier ideas and campaigns of their fellow Missourians Generals William T. Sherman and Ulysses S. Grant, both Pershing and Bradley employed bold movements to win World War I and World War II, via Pershing's offensive in the Argonne and Bradley's breakout, dash across France, and race to conquer Germany.

In many ways, generations of generals also passed on lessons regarding leadership style. The Mexican War was a watershed for Missouri's future generals because it displayed two basic archetypes of effective leadership: Zachary Taylor and Winfield Scott.

Scott, "Old Fuss and Feathers," had the dashing look of a heroic military figure, always neatly dressed and dapper. He tended to stay aloof and remote from his men and never considered himself to be one of them. In contrast, because Taylor, "Old Rough and Ready," dressed like a farmer in blue jeans and a straw hat, he was always one of the men. But no matter how they looked and acted, both generals got results.

Grant served under both Taylor and Scott, but he, and Doniphan, took to Taylor's style of leadership the most. Grant's admiration for Taylor was evident at Appomattox and in his treatment of the defeated Confederates. Doniphan's discipline of his volunteer soldiers was especially lax, but his men performed well when put to the test. Price cared deeply for his men and worked to earn their adoration. As a spit-and-polish, hard-driving disciplinarian, Pershing would fall in the category of a Winfield Scott, while Bradley would be a modern-day disciple of Taylor. Bradley's GI General status would stand in contrast to that of George Patton, who patterned his leadership style after that of his stern, no-nonsense mentor, Pershing.

They were all successful generals. As Mark Twain once said, "It is not the size of the dog in the fight; it's the size of the fight in the dog." "He's a fighter" was Pershing's highest compliment to a subordinate. No matter their outward appearance, these generals knew how to fight.

Yet a general needs to be much more than a fighter. Military leaders also need to be diplomats, administrators, and even politicians. Judging from the careers of the five generals in this book, each played multiple roles in the political realm. Doniphan wrote a constitution for a new state and served in the state legislature. Price was a governor and congressman. Grant was president. Bradley directed the Veterans Administration, and he and Pershing both played significant roles as military advisers to presidents.

In the wars of the twentieth century, the role of the general is most often comparable to that of a manager. This idea emerged under Pershing, but it had been true to some extent since the Civil War. Grant found himself marshaling several armies with differing objectives in different regions of the country to work together to defeat the Confederacy. Pershing, having witnessed the logistical problems that almost made the invasion of Cuba during the Spanish-American War a disaster, used lessons learned the hard way to make sure his American Expeditionary Force in France was a success. Pershing's chief aide and protégé, General George Marshall, would perfect the role of the general as manager, directing the logistics and overall World War II effort from Washington, and Bradley, Marshall's protégé, would implement those management skills on the battlefield in Europe.

But whatever their personality or leadership style, the five Missouri generals included in this book all showed great ability to motivate their troops. They were all leaders who knew how to get the best from their men. Usually successful on the battlefield, they in turn became successful in other pursuits as well. Lessons of leadership learned on the battlefield served them in their later careers as they dealt with the important issues of their times.

For Missourians, these men and their contributions to history should be a source of pride. Some received the adulation or admiration of their men; others were simply respected. But they got the job done and caught the imagination of the public in doing so. Their lives merit study, both to gain a better understanding of history and to learn lessons in leadership.

Index

About the Author

James F. Muench is a public relations consultant and freelance writer. He lives in Columbia, Missouri.